Contesting Childh

p. 36: position + history

visible

Contesting Childhood

Michael G. Wyness

London and New York

First published 2000
by Falmer Press
11 New Fetter Lane, London EC4P 4EE

Simultaneously published in the USA and Canada
by Falmer Press
19 Union Square West, New York, NY 10003

Falmer Press is an imprint of the Taylor & Francis Group

© 2000 Michael G. Wyness

Typeset in Garamond by
M Rules
Printed and bound in Great Britain by
St Edmundsbury Press, Bury St Edmunds, Suffolk

British Library Cataloguing in Publication Data
A catalogue record for this book is available from the British Library

Library of Congress Cataloging in Publication Data
A record for this book has been requested

ISBN 0 750 70824 7 (hbk)
ISBN 0 750 70823 9 (pbk)

To Beth

Contents

Acknowledgements

This book started off life as an article entitled: 'Policy, Protectionism and the Competent Child' and was published in *Childhood: a Global Journal of Child Research*. I must thank the editors for allowing me to expand many of the ideas. A version of chapter 1 was presented at the University of Alberta, as a contribution to the Children and Youth conference in July 1998. It has now been published by Kanata Press within the *Childhood and Youth: a universal odyssey* collection edited by Annette Richardson. I want to thank Annette for her comments and those of the participants.

More generally, various colleagues and friends – Jane Martin, Ian Buchanan, Beth Wykes and Peter Silcock – were kind enough to read drafts of the book. Their comments were invaluable and encouraging. The planning and early drafting of the book took place during a one-term sabbatical granted by my institution, Nene University College, Northampton. I am grateful to my employers for this. Finally, I want to thank Beth for her love and support during a very frantic last few months when the book really started to take shape.

Introduction

As we move towards the new millennium public commentary, social scientific thinking and policy prescriptions continually refer to childhood as a period of physical insecurity and moral ambiguity. The alleged rise in child abuse, the coupling of childhood with crime and disorder and the notion of children's rights are taken as evidence of a failure of adult society to define clearly the moral and social boundaries between themselves and children. In short, there is talk of a crisis of childhood. In this book I argue that that crisis is based on the misplaced idea that childhood is inferior to adulthood. Inferiority here refers to children's imputed inabilities to assume the full range of roles and responsibilities demanded of adults in society. Children's general lack of development in social, moral and emotional terms means that their interests and welfare are determined by their adult counterparts. In other words, what is in crisis is a particular *understanding* of childhood, a recurring set of dominant ideas within political and academic domains that draws a generational boundary between adults and children, in the process restricting children to subordinate and protected social roles.

I claim that this understanding or conception of childhood is in need of serious revision. I argue that within late modern societies boundaries between adults and children are indeed more contested. But rather than interpret this negatively in terms of loss or decline, we should look at it in a positive light: children in some cases have become less reliant on adults and more able to take responsibility for their own affairs. Within this frame of reference children and adults rely less on generational difference as a means of defining their identity. In many contexts and for a variety of reasons, the child as a subordinate subject is a compelling and sometimes necessary conception of modern childhood. In other contexts and for other reasons, children may rely much less on the benevolent patronage of adults. Children may be less subsumed within an adult world of discipline and control because we are more likely now to recognize them as able, willing and reliable contributors within their own significant social contexts of the home and the school. Children may be more active there in negotiating the boundaries between themselves and adults. Rather than think in terms of subordination, we might begin to talk about children as competent social actors.

With reference to these two basic models of childhood, Archard's (1993, pp. 21–23) distinction between *concepts* and *conceptions* of childhood is informative. With reference to a concept of childhood I do not deny the existence of a basic but unspecified notion of separateness between adult and child which may be expressed in terms of status or social position. How this difference is played out between children and adults, the particular form that this concept takes as a conception of childhood, is a product of how we view children from our own peculiar cultural and social vantage points. To talk about a conception is to locate our understandings of childhood within a social, political and cultural context. The implications are that we can talk of different, potentially competing *conceptions* of childhood.

One of the purposes of this book is to spell out the changes, forces and factors that structure our viewpoints of children. But as Hendrick (1997) correctly points out, by 'our' viewpoints we mean the adult perspective; in historical and cultural terms children have played little part in the shaping of their own identities and social positions.[1] One of the dominant themes within recent sociological studies of childhood is the attempt to integrate theoretical understandings of children as active social agents with general analyses of social change that suggest a more informed and confident child population. The contesting of childhood takes place within social scientific circles. The idea of reconstruction here refers to the academy's attempts at reconceptualizing childhood, at examining existing and alternative ideas on childhood based on a range of theoretical and empirical material. The impetus to reconstruct comes from within the academy, but importantly the academy reflects and to some extent informs the broader political and social contexts which children inhabit. Thus, as sociologists and psychologists attempt to relocate childhood outside the conventional conceptual and methodological frameworks of 'socialization' and 'development', frameworks which assume that children are subordinate and dependent, there is an equally difficult task of trying to make sense of children's positions within the shifting networks of relationships and responsibilities that characterize much of late modern society.

In chapter 1 the social and sociological dimensions of childhood are examined with reference to the reconstruction of childhood. Within this framework I will refer to the way childhood is contested at both social and sociological levels. Reconstruction is also articulated in the form of a response to the 'childhood in crisis' theme that has already been mentioned. Crisis works within a restricted theoretical paradigm which presupposes that children are passive recipients of processes of socialization. The social position of children is determined here by the actions of legitimate adult authority figures such as parents and teachers. In chapter 3 I discuss the power of the socialization model in academic, political and professional terms. In chapter 1 I address the possibilities for reframing socialization theory along with the idea of childhood incompetence.

This book also aims to explore differing conceptions of childhood through an analysis of recent social policy. Chapter 2, broadly speaking, examines the relationship between policy reform and childhood. Recent reforms within child care and education policy within Britain are a rich source of material for an analysis of childhood. Child policy generates a complex network of relations between parents, professionals and, in some instances, children which has significant implications for our viewing of childhood. Child policy also follows the same complex patterns of change within the broader society discussed in chapter 1. As with chapter 1 I start by examining the 'crisis of childhood' theme. I examine the way that crisis assumes that policies on child care and education become essential tools in the recovery of childhood. Recent child-care and education reform might be said to strengthen the socializing powers of adults over children. A simple reading of the legislation suggests that political and institutional attempts are being made to reconstruct traditional models of childhood. The major part of chapter 2 is concerned with a rebuttal of this approach. I address the role policy plays in restructuring arrangements made for both the schooling and the protection of children. But rather than see policy as a form of moral rescue, my emphasis here is on the fuzzy and in some cases morally ambiguous relations generated through policy reform between adults with responsibilities for children's welfare, namely, parents and professionals working within educational and child-care fields (the latter hereinafter known collectively as 'child workers'). Social policy is not outside the main social pressures on adults and children: it is not simply a response to social change; it is complicit in the process. Although the child's welfare becomes the centrepiece of child-care policy and practice, there are some grounds for thinking that welfare is an issue that gets subsumed within a network of adult responsibility which obscures and marginalizes the actions of children. Nevertheless, towards the end of the chapter I assess the child's welfare in terms of the way child policy addresses children themselves as influential social actors.

In the book I bring child-care policy and education reform together in suggesting that social policy underpins important changes in the way adults and children relate to each other. These changes shape new ways of thinking about children as well as reaffirming 'old' ways of protecting and restricting them. Although policy reform is not a simple moral response to a crisis relating to childhood, policy nevertheless developed within a backdrop of perceived problems. In chapter 3 I refer to one particular social problem that has developed over the past twenty years and generated a great deal of state activity and public anxiety, the problem of child sexual abuse. The material for this chapter is not drawn directly from child-care policy. There are three reasons for this. First, I broaden the analysis to include legal and professional conceptions of childhood. This means referring to recent policy changes within the criminal justice system. Second, I want to take a broader view on policy. I move away from an interpretation of the child-care legislation *per se* and concentrate on policy contexts and initiatives. Child-care strategies here develop in and around policy, sometimes informally, sometimes in opposition to the broader political trends. Third, I return to the role of the social sciences, particularly the paradigms of socialization and development. Whilst policy makers and practitioners have been busying themselves developing child protection strategies, the knowledge bases to these approaches have become much more contested. From a social scientific point of view, the problem of child abuse seems both to endorse the power and authority of adult protectors and to establish the formative position of children as legal and moral subjects. In chapter 3, then, I address these conflicting views of childhood at policy, research and professional levels.

Chapters 4 and 5 deal with educational matters. In the analysis of the educational context there is a much sharper focus on the conflicting conceptions of childhood. In chapter 4 educational reform is examined explicitly with reference to the status of children in school. The theoretical accent here is on the notion of agency: the general issue revolves around whether there are signs of children's active participation and influence in school matters. More specifically, I pose the question: given the radical import of recent education reform in its transformative effects on most aspects of children's schooling, what effect does this have, if any, on their social status within school? In chapter 5 I examine a range of disparate educational issues which reflect local and global as well as national trends. The dominant theme here is childhood and citizenship. Questions of the child's status are particularly pertinent here. Citizenship has been endlessly debated in the past ten years or so within the social sciences. Questions range from the relative importance of the status of citizen in people's lives to the contested role of the state in structuring our rights as citizens (see Roche, 1992). Citizenship rights rest on the balance of rights and obligations that individuals hold as well as the degree to which people are integrated into the political structures of a society. In one important sense citizenship rights are dependent on rights and obligations being framed around relations between adults and children. The notion of having a stake in society presupposes that adults have moral commitments rooted in a work ethic, particularly in their child-rearing responsibilities. One of the arguments of the book is that this form of 'child-centredness' rooted in recent policy reform is at the heart of the restructuring of adult identities. In chapter 5 I recast some of these questions and debates on citizenship and, at the same time, reconceptualize this child-centredness. Rather than see children as citizens-in-waiting – carefully moulded through the work of fully qualified citizens – I want to assess the extent to which selected educational initiatives address children as more active social agents. In what sense, then, can we start to think of children as citizens?

Although the major focus is British childhood and British social policy the book draws on material from more disparate and global sources. The theoretical and empirical work which underpins the general arguments spans a much broader European and North American base. The policy and 'child-centred' initiatives discussed in chapters 3 and 5 similarly have their origins in North American, Australasian and northern European theory and practice. In chapter 5 the concerns are not only global but have more localized appeal.

A Note on Rights

Although the book is not concerned with the issue of children's rights *per se*, in policy and theoretical terms there is clearly a sense in which an examination of the status of childhood must contend with the question of whether or not children have become more adult-like. The 'childhood in crisis' theme which I discuss in the first two chapters revolves around the notion that children are, in moral and social terms, out of position. The current concerns around children's rights are often blamed for this malaise. Children cannot be expected to accept the unconditional authority of parents if they are encouraged to believe that they have similar political and social standings to those of their parents and teachers (see *The Times*, 30 December 1993).

As I will argue in this book, it is a mistake to conflate children's rights with a loss of position. Children allegedly out of position are accused of 'owning' adult-type rights. A casual perusal of the 'children's rights' literature reveals a clear conflict between *welfare* rights to care and education or, as Franklin and Franklin put it, 'provision and protection' and rights to *self-determination* (1996; see also Freeman, 1983; Archard, 1993). The former strengthens the hold that adults have over children because it works on the assumption that those in authority have an obligation to ensure that rights to health care, education and protection are met on children's behalf. The latter, on the other hand, are far more controversial. Rights to self-determination take certain responsibilities and powers away from adults as children potentially have a right to make decisions for themselves that could potentially go against the interests of adults. These kinds of children's rights do threaten the protective and paternalist roles of adults.

Within the rights discourse childhood is in crisis because children no longer know or accept their place. The conventional rights to self-determination position is occupied by the liberationist or what King calls the 'kiddy libbers' position (1982). The development of these ideas as a social movement in the United States and Great Britain and their specific manifestos and charters have been well documented elsewhere (Freeman, 1983; Franklin and Franklin, 1996). As with any social movement, there is a degree of ideological posturing, particularly over whether children's welfare rights should be strengthened or extended to include rights to self-determination. Yet there is a convergent critique of children's social and political exclusion, which for some leads to a call for a simple and unequivocal reversal of this position through granting children the same rights as adults.

Although I examine two opposing viewpoints on the status of children and childhood – crisis and reconstruction – the children's rights dichotomy between protectionism and liberation does not neatly dovetail. I argue in this book against the crisis thesis and in some important respects this leads to a thorough reappraisal of the protectionist relationship between adult and child. Nevertheless, the reconstruction of childhood – the acceptance of competing understandings of children's social positions – does not necessarily entail a model of the liberated child. Nor do the possibilities for identifying different models of childhood make the claims for children's formal adult status more compelling. For what it is worth, I occupy the middle ground with slight leanings towards loosening the bonds of dependency and patronage. My position is most clearly expressed in chapter 5, where I examine a series of educational initiatives which encourage a more active and informed pupil population. Whilst I do not believe it is desirable or feasible to 'liberate' children, I nevertheless contend that schools, in particular, need to be quite radically restructured with a more democratic, citizen-based ethos.

1 Childhood in Crisis
Decline or Reconstruction?

Introduction

In a recently published article Norbert Elias (1998, p. 16) refers to the 'anachronistic insistence . . . on the family as a simply unchangeable and eternally identical human figuration'. The concern for bedrock social and moral certainties – their dissolution and attempted resurrection – has led some social commentators to identify 'the family' and its disappearance as a primary source of social breakdown. Elias (1998) goes on to argue that this is an insistence on the nuclear family. This view obscures any realistic understanding of the range of problems that family members currently face. In effect, he is saying that as social analysts we need to move beyond a nuclear frame of reference and address the possibility that individuals arrange their domestic lives in qualitatively different ways.

What Elias is pointing out is the way in which commentators reaffirm a single nuclear version of family within a social context where the nuclear family becomes increasingly less relevant. We can draw a parallel between this alleged crisis of 'the family' and the purported crisis of childhood. Just as diagnoses and prescriptions are expounded within a nuclear family frame irrespective of the particular problems faced by parents and children, so problems such as delinquency, video nasties and sex abuse are examined with reference to an undifferentiated model of the child which takes little account of the concrete circumstances of different groups of children. Social scientists, policy makers and 'child workers' draw on theories, principles and speculations based on a dominant conception of childhood made up of characteristics such as innocence, naïvety and vulnerability. Moreover, a single conception of childhood becomes a reference point for the evaluation of children's behaviour and those institutions and individuals who have responsibilities towards children.

Of late, much of this evaluation of childhood has converged on the idea that it is in crisis. To simplify matters, I want to argue that this 'crisis' rests on the idea that children are out of place. This can be taken literally to mean that children are less likely to be found within the adult-regulated confines of the home and school. We can also think of it in the metaphorical sense that children are more challenging and less subservient, less likely to accept the unconditional nature of relations with parents and teachers, in other words, children's social positions can no longer be taken for granted. Some might conclude from this that children's attitudes and behaviour no longer conform to a 'universal and natural' model of childhood. For many this is tantamount to saying that childhood has disappeared.

An alternative way of viewing childhood is to suspend judgement on the contemporary condition of childhood on the grounds that problems and crises attributed to children can be recast in terms of social change. There is then less need to rescue childhood, for the 'universal and natural' conception of childhood is less relevant now. We need to reframe the circumstances within which childhood is found to be in trouble and concentrate more on how children and childhood might be changing. Children and childhood, then, need to be reconceptualized, some might say reconstructed. At the very least we need to attempt to understand the changing nature of children's lives and examine the possibility of more contested versions of childhood. From this point of view we might speculate that children rely less on generational difference as a reference point for self-identity. We might pursue this point further. Children are less likely to be treated as subjects to be disciplined and controlled than they were, say, during the post-war period because we are more likely to view them now as competent social actors who participate in the shaping of their social environments.

The purpose of this chapter is to examine crisis and reconstruction as two dominant themes within the sociology of childhood. In the first part I will argue that the problem of childhood not only parallels the 'loss of family' refrain but appears to be deeply implicated in the problem of family. I thus address crisis, first of all, with reference to the alleged breakdown in family relations. I go on to examine a second key element within the 'crisis of childhood' thesis: the diminution of the child's world of play. In the second part I explore the possibilities of reframing childhood within theories of late modernity. Although existing work on late modernity offers few possibilities for the reconceptualizing of childhood, I will outline the key themes that run through the 'new sociology of childhood', which have strong family resemblances to theories of late modernity. I address relatively recent attempts to reposition the child conceptually and empirically. Three areas are addressed: (a) the socially constructed nature of childhood, (b) the problem of the invisible child and (c) the recognition of childhood in terms of social agency.

Childhood in Crisis

Decline of Family and Authority

I referred earlier to a set of popular descriptions of childhood. Sociologists have drawn on the characteristics of naïvety, corruptibility and innocence in defining the child as a social incompetent who needs to be brought to a state of sociability and morality through the benevolent authority of parents, ideally those within the nuclear family (Parsons, 1965). The crisis of childhood in these terms rests on the assumption that the problem lies not within the child but in the way the child is socialized. Parents are no longer able to provide the moral and social resources which propel the child out into society. The process of socialization becomes increasingly difficult because parents fail to establish secure moral and social boundaries for their children. Children themselves illustrate this failure in the way that they behave and in their attitude to a whole range of things. As the Newsons comment,

> Parents are in fact chronically on the defensive over their parental role because the responsibility laid on them is not only limitless but supremely personal. Our children are a walking testimonial or advertisement for the sort of people we are; doubly so, since they advertise both heredity and their environment [*sic*].
> (Cited in Harris, 1983, p. 240)

In my earlier work with families, I have commented on the way some parents articulated difficulties they had with their children in terms of relative 'powerlessness' or a general decline in adult authority, particularly within the home and school (Wyness, 1997). Now I am not attempting here to provide illustrative evidence of the 'childhood in crisis' theme, for there were other parents who took a more agnostic line in viewing adult–child relations in terms of *change* rather than decline, views incidentally that bring us closer to the idea of reconstruction, an alternative interpretation of modern childhood discussed later in the chapter. Nevertheless, there does seem to be a growing set of popular beliefs that children no longer conform quite so easily to the rosy post-war images of childhood and the nuclear family. The press coverage of a recent case of a 12-year-old boy taking his father to court for 'smacking' him provides an example of this. The headline for *The Times* read 'Boy denied glory of seeing his father tried for smacking' (4 September 1996, p. 11). The case did not go to court, according to the author, on the basis of evidence admitted to the Crown Prosecution Service by a doctor. It is worth quoting the report:

> [The solicitor] for the teacher [the father], said: 'He was simply administering lawful and reasonable chastisement'. The incident had been referred to a number of doctors, one of whom said the boy was 'a 12 year old who will bask in the glory of his accusations' and that it would be an unmitigated disaster for the family.

The implicit message here is of a precocious child irresponsibly invoking his rights against his father, his guardian and socializer, with family break-up a possible outcome. The position of the child, the parent–child relationship and the child's perceived ability to draw on the state in bringing the parent in line are key elements in my analysis of adult–child relations in this and the following chapters. For the purposes of this chapter and the following section, I address sociological treatments of family and the institution of childhood from quite ideologically diverse perspectives. In what follows I want to address the problem of childhood and family from differing political viewpoints. Let us begin with the problem as seen from a right-wing vantage point.

We can trace the current critique of family and childhood to the early 1970s with the publication of the Black Papers, a series of critical commentaries on the comprehensive system of schooling in Britain. The central concern running through these pamphlets and books was the alleged decline in curricular and pedagogic 'standards' in British state schools. But the proponents of educational change took families and politicians to task for an alleged decline in standards of behaviour among the young. As one prominent critic asserted:

> children are growing up in a welfare state where it appears that everything in school is free: it is a world where they follow their inclinations and where things are not right or wrong but merely a matter of opinion and where there are virtually no rules.
>
> (Johnson, 1971, p. 99)

Judgements here are sweeping in attributing blame at the level of the state, the family and the classroom. But the fundamental problem, at least with reference to an alleged decline in behavioural standards, appears to lie with the inadequate role that adults play in structuring children's moral and social development. Adults are no longer willing or able to provide children with clear moral guidelines. The adjective 'permissive' normally precedes a description of parenting and the position of teachers and, in a broader sense, the character of British and American culture.

More recently, this theme has run through Charles Murray's critique of family life (1990). Despite its moral connotations, the imputation of blame seems to be the analytical strategy adopted by Murray in identifying a breakdown in family relations. Blaming families draws him into identifying particular types of families found within what has been termed the underclass. Imported from the American inner cities via a series of articles in *The Times*, Murray's version of the underclass chimes with the political concerns over the cost of the 'dysfunctional family' to the state. According to this thesis, certain sectors of the population are culpable in creating a culture of deprivation and crime. Parents, in particular, are singled out for their inability to control or discipline their children. Economic variables such as income and unemployment are less significant as Murray seeks to draw the nineteenth-century distinction between the 'deserving' and 'undeserving' poor. The underclass becomes the late twentieth-century version of the undeserving poor because their poverty is based on behaviour and lifestyle. In other words, members of the underclass are blamed for their drug taking, their criminal propensities, their rejection of work and, most important of all, their rejection of marriage because they choose these courses of action.

What is most worrying for Murray is how this lack of moral guidelines within underclass families affects children. '[L]ittle boys [were not] naturally growing up to be responsible fathers and husbands . . . and little girls don't become adolescents naturally wanting to refrain from having babies' (1990, p. 10). Children are not children within the underclass because parents do not exercise a 'natural' authority over them. The suggestion here is that underclass children fall outside the normal nuclear model of childhood. They are less subject to strong moral imperatives from parents. They are more exposed to the negative features of the adult world and exhibit all the hallmarks of the 'precocious child' or the 'adult-child'. In these terms we can make sense of recent concerns over the 'youthfulness' of delinquency and the problems of children committing adult-like crimes. The child criminal is associated with the broader problem of the decline in adult authority.

The teenage mother, particularly the single teenage mother, in the ambiguous role of the adult-child, is another familiar reference point in the analysis of the underclass and the breakdown of family. The reproduction of the underclass rests on the 'cycle of poverty' thesis whereby parents transmit a culture of poverty to the next generation (Lewis, 1967). Young men and women learn little about moral commitment in that they are more likely to reject the moral requirements of sexual relations. Teenage mothers detached from the fathers of their children in turn provide few appropriate moral reference points for their children, as well as consigning themselves and their children to a life of welfare dependency. Yet within this school of thought the teenage mother is both a potent and ambiguous symbol of the undeserving poor. She is less likely to be formally accepted as a member of a disadvantaged group entitled to state support because of her membership of the underclass and her status as a child. There is an inconsistency here between the teenage mother as an irresponsible adult who has no moral right to welfare support and the teenage mother – particularly under the age of 16 – as a child inappropriately engaging in sex who no longer fits the dominant conception of childhood in terms of family dependency and innocence.

In her perceptive critique of the American political right, Pearce argues that pregnancy may be a rational *adult* choice for many young working-class women (1993). Yet public campaigns deny the teenage mother a degree of voluntarism because they address teenage motherhood in the emotive terms of 'children having children'. Pearce claims that this moral position is backed by institutional support. There are difficulties in setting up clinics for teenage mothers because this is perceived to be encouraging adolescent sexual activity. She also contends that public policy enforces teenage mothers' dependency on their parents by making it difficult for them to set up separate households, by restricting their claims for income support and by forcing them to return to school as soon as possible after the birth of the child.

Many of these concerns can be identified within a left-wing standpoint. But whereas the right think in terms of reasserting a 'purer' form of capitalism, the left see that solution to the restoration of childhood as the source of its decline. They argue that the by-products of capitalism – consumerism and privatization – have superseded parents as cultural frames of reference for children. In an earlier text, Jeremy Seabrook (1982) invokes a romanticized notion of working-class community life that incorporates both a strong sense of the child's position within the nuclear family and the idea of separateness from the adult world. The loss of childhood here rests on the shift from an emotional and moral axis of support from parent to child to the material excesses of a consumer society. Parents, in effect, become victims of the market because, in the absence of moral commitment, they are forced to rely on their children's material dependency, the only remaining hold that they have over their children. Parents buy their children's respect by supplying them with the necessary accoutrements such as computers and trainers that keep their children ahead of their peers in the competition for social esteem.

In a recent paper, 'Children of the market' (1998), Seabrook explores the issues from the child's perspective. Taking a global line, he divides children into the unprotected and undernourished victims of the developing southern hemisphere, and, in the advanced North, victims of a satiated and overnourished market. Importantly, the latter are also victims of the alleged breakdown of family:

> With almost half the marriages in the US ending in divorce, with the decay of even the nuclear family, the recreation of temporary units of half-brothers and sisters and step-mothers and fathers and 'Mum's boyfriend' or 'Dad's girlfriend', a terrible insecurity and anxiety are created in children, a sense of perishability of human relationships. In this context, the world of what money will buy, even the fleeting, evanescent world of fashionable garments, items of wear that will be discarded within a few months or weeks, comes to look more solid, more reliable than human ties and relationships of blood and bone.
>
> (1998, p. 45)

In an earlier article, Harris (1977) refers to this as the development of the implosive family, an unstable set of relations between family members. He refers to two forms: the disintegrated family and the child-centred family. The former is characterized by minimal contact between members, with the home functioning more as a hotel. The latter, which Harris argues is more common, rests on the inversion of the dependency relationship with parents' sense of self almost exclusively determined by their children.[1] Harris sees this as a form of child-centredness – an unhealthy dependency on the child; the vicarious development of meaningful adult identities through the process of child rearing; the disproportionate amount of time, money and emotional energy invested in the children (Harris, 1983). In both cases the implosion is a product of late capitalism which denies adults any real intrinsic satisfactions as either workers or parents.

With the rise in individualism and calculation in the 1980s in Britain many public utilities have been sold off into private hands. Marina Warner (1989) draws a parallel between the privatizing of resources such as water, gas and electric supplies which had previously been in state hands and the idea that childhood has been privatized in such a way that children, a common commodity, enter the language of the market as a scarce resource, in the demographic and economic senses. Population trends point to smaller families across the socio-economic spectrum. Yet choice, the new social reference point for investing in children, is monopolized by the affluent middle classes. Warner refers to the way working-class mothers, particularly single and teenage ones, are targeted by the political right in terms of their propensity to breed, which is supposed to reflect their dissolute lifestyles. At the other end of the spectrum, families allegedly imbued with what may be considered an economically thriftier mentality view their children as prospective private assets. Thus, unlike Murray who attributes 'choice' to the underclass as a means of differentiating individualistic from deterministic explanations of parental inadequacy, for Warner it is middle-class parents who 'choose' to have children on the basis of value and cost.

A final comment on left-wing thinking on family and childhood brings us to those who seem to have close moral as well as intellectual ties with the political right, the self-appointed 'ethical socialists'. In the case of Dennis and Erdos (1992) the convergence rests on the 'absent father' thesis which asserts that the working classes have become more irresponsible and criminal because of a rise in the number of boys born into lone-parent households. Again there is reference to the weakening of moral ties within families and the spectre of the man-child, the boy with no male adult figure hovering above him to constrain and regulate his precocious appetites. Melanie Phillips, in her regular newspaper articles and book *All Must Have Prizes* (1996), makes similar claims by drawing on the figure of the 'disordered child'. Recurring themes such as 'prematurely sexualised children', the 'flight from parenting' and the 'no blame, no shame, no pain society' indicate an alleged moral malaise rooted in a selfish individualism and adult society's inability to exercise authority over children. Children are disordered because they are not acted upon. To be sure, this lack of determinism for some children is rooted in forms of neglect and a lack of love and attention. But there is also an absence of moral commitment on the part of parents to define clearly and unambiguously the position that children must occupy until they are judged to be ready to make their own decisions. Children are thus disordered in the sense both being out of control and of being out of position within the social hierarchy.

From Marbles to Video Games: the Commodification of Play

'The family' is taken as one frame of reference for the analysis of childhood. Others have sought to identify children in their 'natural' state where they are physically separate from adults. Play is taken to symbolize spontaneity and the unmediated world of nature. It offers a context within which children exhibit their childish tendencies as well as suggesting a time scale for the separation of children from the adult world of work (James, Jenks and Prout, 1998). Play is also a world that children temporarily inhabit whilst they are gradually introduced to the formalism of the wider social world through the school. According to Hengst (1987) and Suransky (1982) there is a necessary tension between the more structured curricular activities found in the classroom and the innocent but sometimes brutal manoeuvres on the playground. This tension or dialectic is supposed to work its way through childhood to be eventually resolved by the time children reach adulthood. Crisis here has arisen because the child's ability to resolve this dialectic has been gradually eroded by the dynamics of industrialization.

> Childhood is being liquidated because today society is invading all those areas in which formerly children had been trained to meet the qualitatively different demands of adulthood. The gap between the generations is narrowing because important segments of reality either have come largely to coincide (as in leisure-time activities), or different spheres of experience (such as school and job) are similarly structured and call forth comparable appropriation processes and 'survival strategies'. As society comes to influence individuals directly through a multitude of channels and agencies, the processes of upbringing, in particular, increasingly lose their effectiveness, are neutralised, and no longer yield intended effects.
>
> (Hengst, 1987, p. 74)

The argument touches on the Marxist approach discussed earlier, in the way that capitalism as a form of industrialism no longer holds out the possibility for more spontaneous and 'natural' relations between children and their parents and children and their peers. Children's play is thus lost under the continual pressure for children to conform to the demands of industrial society.

In his ethnography of American schooling, Wexler (1992, p. 65) identifies these pressures, particularly among middle-class children, with teachers and parents channelling pupils' energies towards academic success. This has the effect of emptying the 'social centre [within schools] in the pursuit of academic excellence'. Schooling here takes an extreme form of individualism. One student from Wexler's sample claims: 'we have always been taught to abandon childhood, go ahead and form more advanced and subtle ways of thinking' (1992, p. 57). Wexler points to the negative effects on pupils such as strain, anxiety and a sense of failure.

The same preoccupation with children's work is identified by authors outside a European and North American context. In Cho Hae-Joang's (1995) analysis of South Korean childhood, children from an early age become almost addicted to studying for exams. In her analysis of the Japanese education system, Norma Field (1995) emphasizes the need to protect Japanese childhood from 'bondage to an overdetermined future'. She argues that Japanese society's interest in a disciplined workforce has eroded any notion of childhood as a period of relative autonomy and play. Children from a very early age are pushed in the manner of the exceptionally gifted child, the prodigy. Driven by a 'schooling industry' and the aspirations of Japanese parents, children spend the greater part of their lives trying to be successful in school. Field refers to cramming in the evenings, endless testing and the burgeoning market in textbooks and manuals.

The disappearance of play has also been identified at the point when children are quintessentially identified with nature, the pre-school period. Suransky (1982) refers to the way that work disciplines shape the child's life at a much earlier age. From her observations of day-care centres in the USA, she argues that the structuring of pre-school children's activities according to child-centred philosophies has the paradoxical effect of reducing the world of play to adult-centred concerns for structure and control. She characterizes one day-care centre as a 'training ground for the early bureaucratization of children' (1982, p. 106). Children's play here becomes more responsive to curricular demands. In other words, pre-school children's use of time and space is much more regulated in terms of theories of child development. Interestingly, we catch a glimpse of the child's world relatively free of adult regulation when she compares the typical regulated day centre with a less structured environment. In the latter case the centre is organized on more communal and spontaneous grounds where there is little timetabling, where activities are more open-ended and merged together. In short, a situation where children are allowed to be children because of the unplanned and spontaneous nature of their activities. Play, according to this scenario, is corrupted as it becomes a specific form of investment for adults. Children are thus not allowed to develop an understanding of the world through play on their own terms and are denied the relatively autonomous space of childhood.

The crisis of childhood is articulated in terms of the relative absence of time, space and opportunity for children to play. But it is also expressed in the way that children's play has been absorbed into the adult world of leisure. The problem here is that children's play is not sufficiently different or separate from adults' 'play'. The lack of spontaneity and the structuring of children's leisure time is a key theme running through

Postman's (1982) polemic on childhood. If we take the example of football, children no longer play in a desultory fashion in any available space
on the street or the park. Football is now organized as matches based very
closely on professional 'adult' models where children's progress on the
field is more closely scrutinized and supervised (1982, p. 128). Football
here becomes a form of leisure-time grid referencing in which children
pick up very early the professional and cynical tactics of competing as
well as thinking solely in terms of winning. In similar vein, Winn (1983,
p. 63) identifies a shift within children's literature from around the
1950s onwards. Rather than constructing a world of fantasy through
fairy-tales, children are now more likely to subscribe to satirical maga-
zines such as *MAD*, which are seen as scaled-down versions of adult
entertainment.

Postman also looks at how children's play has changed through the
introduction of electronic media. The development of mass media over
the past fifty years, in particular the role of television and advertising, has
opened up the ostensibly adult worlds of sex, violence and economics to
children. Children, according to this argument, have become more adult-
like because the separate world of children's play has been invaded by
mass media that address the child as a cynical calculating consumer.
Television, in particular, comes in for a great deal of criticism for breaking down the boundaries between adults and children. Postman argues
that new educational ideologies and technologies can no longer sustain
the crucial distance between the adult and child's world. This approach
thus makes no concession for 'educational viewing' such as *Blue Peter* and
Sesame Street (1982, pp. 77–80). No matter what the content of television
is, no matter that 'children's viewing' may be prescribed according to
strict developmental maxims, television as a 'world of simultaneity and
instancy' (p. 70) puts children on a par with adults in that information
about the world which was previously monopolized by parents and
teachers is now accessible to children. Television as it were extinguishes
any secrets that adults had.

Postman emphasizes the boundary between adult and child through
the concept of shame. Children have to learn to repress certain feelings
and modes of behaviour. Children learn to be civil through a mixture of
formal and informal interactions, with adults. Adults exercise a power
over children, a power that resides in the secretion of information about
how to behave – how not to 'shame' themselves. This information is
given out to children gradually as they move towards adulthood. For
Postman television not only erodes the boundary between child's play
and adult entertainment, it symbolizes the erosion of adult authority
over children.

Some interesting comments on the decline of child's play can be found in Corsaro's (1997) analysis of children's cultures. Corsaro provides three reasons for arguing that '[k]ids seem to have less time to be kids' (ibid., p. 38). First, there is the parental need to protect children, based on their perception of the outside world as an alien environment populated by folk devils such as paedophiles and roving gangs of delinquents. Parents are more likely to organize their children's free time around activities which give them more direct control and bring them within their purview. This reduces the opportunity that children have for more spontaneous play with their peers away from the immediate vicinity of parents. I will discuss the protectionist impulses of adults in later chapters. The point that I want to make here is that the need to let children explore the social world on their own through play is, according to the crisis approach, overridden by the need to protect children from moral and physical danger (Wyness, 1994). A second factor relates to the rising numbers of dual earning families placing their children in public care centres. In Britain, the introduction of after-school clubs has become increasingly significant in absorbing children's leisure time. Two things might compromise this as children's time: after-school clubs take place at times when children might be expected to play with their peers and thus are more likely to be seen as an extension of school. A second point follows: adults with responsibilities for 'baby-sitting' these children will inevitably generate more regulatory pressures on the children than, say, the child's carers within the home. This may not extend to pedagogic relations with children but given more general protectionist impulses and the need to scrutinize closely all non-family activities with children (to be discussed in subsequent chapters), child's play becomes much more regulated by adults. Finally, Corsaro draws on Hector Hernandez's work on the changing demographic situation, particularly in North America. He refers to a significant shift from large to small families throughout most of the twentieth century. This has meant that children become progressively less reliant on siblings to introduce them into the public sphere. Again, according to Corsaro, adults become more prominent sources of social support because there are fewer opportunities to form alliances with other children and play within the relatively autonomous sphere of the peer group.

To sum up: the 'childhood in crisis' theme rests on the decline of two key features of childhood, the bounded nuclear family and the world of play. Theorists here present us with a peculiarly western, restricted and not always consistent version of childhood. The crisis of childhood is both paralleled by and implicated in the decline of the nuclear family.

Children are no longer children because they are now less likely to be 'nucleated', that is, controlled and nurtured under the watchful, hopeful eyes of a morally and socially united mother/father unit. At the same time the little degree of autonomy that children are granted – the residual space of the playground and park – has now all but disappeared as adults seek to regulate all aspects of the child's social world in the interests of a political and economic sphere that makes ever-increasing demands for a more disciplined and productive workforce. Thus play is sacrificed in the interests of profit maximization; spontaneity and innocence are replaced with regulation and bureaucracy. Children then are less childlike because they can no longer be neatly positioned within family and peer group, institutions and structures that typify the essential characteristics of childhood.

The Contested Nature of Childhood

The Limits of Individualization

When we consider the theories of late or post-modernity, at first glance there would appear to be ample room for the reconceptualizing of childhood. Social structural changes are linked to a diverse range of cultural forms ranging from new social movements (Giddens, 1990) to a resurgent individualism (Beck, 1992). In particular, the work of Ulrich Beck (1987, 1992) suggests the frames of reference associated with economic growth and technological progress such as social class, nation and community are being replaced by processes of individualization. The implication here is that individuals are relatively freer now to construct their social identity through concepts such as risk and opportunity. According to this thesis, members of all social classes are now more likely to make decisions with long-term 'biographical' consequences. Individuals are confronted with a wider range of choices (opportunities) without the insurance of modernist frames of reference (the increase in risk). Thus women are less constrained by gender because they can now contemplate the idea of a professional career. Social class becomes a less compelling reference point as more and more people are encouraged to become property owners and the great educational class divide is compromised by a plethora of choices open to young people when they leave school.

Various criticisms have been made of this thesis on theoretical and methodological grounds.[2] Nevertheless, the logic of this theory is worth pursuing for it implies that close personal affinities as well as economic and social relations have been transformed. Beck refers to the nuclear family, a dominant site of childhood, being affected by the processes of individualization. We may be forgiven for thinking that this theory would render concepts such as tradition, shame and authority redundant. But the focus is on the changing nature of relations between adults, in particular the replacement of the sexual division of labour with more flexible forms. There is, importantly, very little on how individualization challenges the boundaries between parents and children. Individualization, if anything, serves to strengthen existing ties between adults and children. For Beck (1992, p. 118), 'the child is the last *remaining irrevocable, unexchangeable primary relationship*. Parents come and go. The child stays. Everything that is desired, but not realizable in the relationship, is directed to the child [author's emphasis]'. Social roles and responsibilities are in a state of flux, yet children are somehow insulated from the effects of late modernity. Beck seems to be arguing that childhood is the last bastion of a disappearing modern order. There is here the same feeling of 'implosion' discussed earlier. There is also a naïvety, almost a romanticism, in Beck's argument that within a context of social chaos and moral uncertainty, adults cling to the belief that at the end of the day children will still rely on them as their primary source of material and emotional support. What we come up against here is the well-worn limits to individualism, the status of the child as a dependent incompetent. The child cannot experience social disorder or moral anxiety for the child is neither social nor moral. Importantly, the child cannot take up the opportunities, of liberation and choice that individualization offers for the child is not an active social agent.

One recent empirical attempt at going beyond the conventional limits to individualization is the work of Leena Alanen (1998). Despite the small size of her sample of one-parent families from four Nordic countries, she challenges the notion that children are completely dependent on their parents. In emphasizing the formative role that some of the children play within these families, she is identifying the way in which children have an influence on the daily routines which have traditionally been organized by parents. Alanen's work points in the general direction of a broader shift in relations between adults and children. She draws on Buchner's version of individualization whereby there is more emphasis on 'the redistribution of family and non-family influences' (Buchner, 1990, p. 78). Buchner refers to the increasing importance of peer-group 'leisure' activities compared with the traditional dependency ties found within the family. Importantly, both authors directly counter the 'disappearance of childhood' thesis. Buchner refers to the way in which this new-found involvement in the leisure field gives children a greater degree of autonomy and a much stronger position within the market-place as consumers. Alanen's work points to the greater possibilities for negotiating generational boundaries because of the specific nature of the families studied. Yet without a comparison of two-parent house-holds this point is difficult to sustain. What is significant about Alanen's study is that she contradicts the idea that the growth of one-parent fam-ilies can only be understood as an indicator of social decline. Instead, she argues that this family type is part of a broader pattern of social change whereby social positions are more fluid and contested and where chil-dren's contributions within the home are valued as integral parts of the domestic economy. Irrespective of whether one-parent families produce more 'agentic' children, her study is part of a broader attempt to move sociology's emphasis on the nuclear family as a centrifugal force towards a frame of reference where families reflect more complex gender and generational relations.

Chris Jenks (1996) explicitly locates childhood within late modernity. He argues that recent issues such as child abuse, child crime and chil-dren's rights reflect the current concern for identity and security. These issues generate differing and potentially competing conceptions of child-hood. According to Jenks, this is problematic for social commentators, policy experts and child-care professionals, for there is now no definitive model of childhood to guide them, no real sense in which any particular combination of care, control or, for that matter, liberation can deal with the perceived problems relating to childhood. The immediate aftermath of the murder of Jamie Bulger, a 2-year-old boy, by two 10-year-old boys in England illustrates this confusion in two ways. First there was a public clamour for the child-offenders to be treated against type as adults in the forms of punishments to be administered to them. Second, the Bulger murder seemed to bring to the surface the emotional 'implosion' discussed earlier. Not only was the public calling for retribution, but there was greater concern voiced over surveillance both of children as potential victims and offenders in public and private spheres.[3] Young children were to be harnessed, literally and metaphorically. Adults became obsessed with keeping their children close, particularly in public places like shopping centres. To take one example, in the immediate aftermath of the Bulger court case plans were drawn up to install an elec-tronic tagging system in a Scottish shopping centre to prevent young children from being abducted (*Sunday Times*, 21 November 1993, p. 3). The idea here was that small electronic devices were to be attached to a child's clothing which were triggered if the child left the shopping centre. We can put some of these 'innovations' down to the immediate public reaction to the case. Yet, five years on, the emphasis still seems to be on protection and control rather than any notion of the child as a self-determining agent.

Constructing Childhood

With the exception of Chris Jenks, few theorists of late or post-modernity have been prepared to follow through the logic of their arguments in terms of the 'individualization' of childhood.[4] We have to turn to more recent substantive work within what might be termed the new sociology of childhood to find any significant reassessments of the social position of the child. A first point to make is that the focus within this new body of work shifts from the child as a biological entity to the child as a social construction. Now it is worth taking a slight detour here to point out that, although many of the arguments around the idea of the disappearing child rest on more fixed biological assumptions, the work of Postman, who is held up as a chief exponent of the decline thesis, rests on the socially produced idea of childhood. His argument follows from the seminal work of Aries (1961) on the historical character of childhood. Aries was concerned with the historical shift in sentiments which shaped a set of ideas and values that gradually crystallized into the idea of the modern child. In Postman's case technological change is the driving force behind changes to the way in which adults think about children. In an important sense both were pointing to the socially constructed nature of childhood. Yet, because they seemed to suggest the gradual unfolding of modern childhood, their arguments take on an essentialist character in their insistence on the rise and, in Postman's case, fall of a modern western notion of the child. What we have here is the unfolding of a universal concept of childhood. If we concentrate on Postman because he discusses the fall of childhood, his critique of modern culture and the consequent collapse of the boundary between child and adult presupposes that all children in all cultures are more or less susceptible to the demoralizing influences of the mass media. More will be made of this in the following chapters, but it is worth pointing to a welter of anthropological work and other social scientific analyses of children in different parts of the world to make the point that Postman's case possibly holds only in a televisual culture such as the United States (see Boyden, 1997).

The clearest statement on the socially constructed nature of childhood can be found in Wendy and Rex Stainton Rogers' (1992) *Stories of Childhood.* The title of their book does not suggest that the story-teller is accounting for a material entity the child who is situated, as it were, outside the story. The story in a sense *is* the child or, in sociological terms, the discourse constitutes the child. Unlike the 'crisis' thesis, childhood is not some ever-present universal entity. It is a product of theories, ideas and debate normally situated within the academic, professional and political spheres. Now these accounts or discourses are normally situated within social time and space in such a way that we are able to identify 'childhood' historically and culturally. Logically, given that there are differences within and between societies in values, understandings and organizational principles, the child may be seen very differently depending on the social setting. The socially constructed child is bounded by particular cultures and histories. In this provisional sense, we can talk about different, possibly contesting notions of childhood.

Although the social constructionist approach is important in that it establishes the cultural dimensions of childhood, it is worth drawing attention to its limitations. First, childhood as a social construction has led to a degree of relativism. For Qvortrup (1994, p. 4) this leads to the 'preponderance of what is unique over what is common'. If childhood is too heavily tied to context, then logically there is very little that can be said in a general sense about the nature of childhood. Moreover, in dealing with the politics of childhood at both global and national levels, this approach cannot really account for more universal notions such as the child's needs or the child's welfare. Although work has been done to 'deconstruct' these notions, cultural specificities would tend to obscure the possibility of uncovering conditions and problems that most children face at a global level.

A second and related difficulty with social constructionism is the absence of any clear guidelines for identifying common features of childhood. Several authors have tried to establish childhood objectively in terms of 'structural' characteristics, with children usually positioned as an exploited and inferior social group. Qvortrup (1994) promotes the idea that childhood ought to be seen as a permanent feature of societies, which would bring it in line with other social categories such as class and 'race'. Hood-Williams (1990) draws on feminist theory and the concept of patriarchy in arguing that children, like women, are a social group that has been systematically excluded from spheres of social, economic and political interest. Other feminists have been critical of the broad trend within feminist thought for childhood to be collapsed within the broader category of gender oppression. Whilst the same sources of tension can be found in adult–child and male–female relations, Thorne (1993) argues that children make up a separate exploited class and explores the possibilities for women as well as men to treat children as a subordinate social grouping.

Oldman (1994), on the other hand, takes a Marxist line in seeing children as a separate social class economically exploited by a superior adult class through the notion of 'child work'. Here adults work on children within a range of different contexts. Oldman draws on the 'defamilialization' of childhood in strengthening his case that child work, because it increasingly takes place outside the home, has a more objective economic value. Thus the increasing specialization of paid work within child-care, child-protection and educational contexts reinforces the conceptual possibility for grounding adult–child relations as economic relations, with children providing employment for adults which strengthens the economic power of adults at the cost of children's own interests.

The Invisible Child

Despite the limitations of constructionism, there does seem to be some common ground between the 'constructionists' and 'objectivists' in relation to the problem of the child's invisibility. If we continue with the Stainton Rogers' 'story of childhood' we are continually confronted with one story of childhood, an account largely constructed by academics and policy experts referred to by the Stainton Rogers as the 'the masonry of the mature' (1992, p. 146). This story rests on the notion of the child as a fixed material object with little or no social status. The child is invisible, first of all, because the dominant 'story' of childhood denies children an ontology. As Jenks argues, '[M]ost social theories through their emphasis on a taken for granted adult world, signally fail to constitute "the child" as an ontology in its own right' (Jenks, 1982, pp. 13–14). According to this dominant account, childhood is a transitional phase which is only complete once children enter adulthood. In an important sense the child is an adult in waiting and therefore not part of the social world that counts. In part this story is sustained because childhood is associated with nature and biology, a primordial and a-social stage of being. The story is similar to the dominant account of childhood told within the 'crisis' approach. Children are supposed to become progressively more visible as they move towards adulthood. If we refer back to the outline of the crisis approach, images conjured up by Charles Murray (1989) on the underclass connote children out of place and out of time because of a breakdown within families, which are supposed to structure this gradual coming out of children, or what has been more commonly called a 'coming of age'. The alleged loss of authority and the abdication of responsibility within families have propelled children into places and positions before they are ready. We are presented with the image of the man-child, the demonic precocious deviant who has become all too readily visible. 'Visibility' here signifies a problem for society.

Second, children's social invisibility means that, in the literal and metaphorical sense, children do not count (Qvortrup, 1997). Statistically, children are hidden within more socially significant institutions such as family, household or school. They are normally counted as 'dependants' and excluded as a unit of reference. Statistical invisibility is reflected in other spheres. Children are not counted because they are not expected to have a stake in the present social, economic or political arrangements. They do not vote, cannot claim an income and are judged not to play any recognized formative role within school or home. Having said this, policy makers are starting to recognize children's absence from social and political fields. The recent Children Act in Britain and the 1989 United Nations Convention of the Rights of the Child are legal attempts to reposition the child. More will be said about these innovations in later chapters. But despite these innovations, children's structural invisibility still seems to be reflected in the way that institutions and politicians are by and large not accountable to children.

In the following chapters I will address this invisibility in more detail. According to the new sociology of childhood, the concept of the child becomes an important focus of analysis because research and theorizing are now bringing to light the hidden nature of children's lives. Research draws on the broader political project of recognizing children's rights and interests, thus rendering children visible within the public sphere. One of the main themes of this book is that children's structural invisibility still seems to be reflected in the way that institutions and politicians are by and large still expected to make decisions on behalf of children, grounded in the notion of knowing what is in the child's 'best interest'. Yet we can identify some technical and policy innovations on childhood which have fed into more 'child-centred' social scientific research. The work of Qvortrup and his colleagues on the European-wide Children as a Social Phenomenon project has been instrumental in generating inter-est in children at the statistical level – see, for example, the recent publication in Britain of statistics relating exclusively to children, *Social Focus on Children* (1994).

Childhood and Agency

A third feature of the new sociology of childhood is the need to explore the possibilities of children as active and competent members of society. A recognition of the child's full social status follows from the idea that children are capable of making sense of their social environment and that it is no longer appropriate to consign childhood to marginal cognitive and moral categories. As Prout and James succinctly argue, children, rather than being 'passive subjects of social structures', are active in shaping their social identities and those others around them (1997, p. 8).

The new sociology of childhood seems to leave open differing possibilities for linking childhood to agency. Here we return to the split between constructing childhood and locating children within the existing social structure. For some researchers the issue is of asserting children's competence within their own delimited worlds of childhood. The influence of interactionist and phenomenological approaches suggests that life worlds and meanings are private. Thus what children say or do is understood in terms of the private meanings and life worlds of children. Methodologically speaking, the emphasis is on identifying agency through the analysis of small-scale interactions and settings which act like micro-societies. The work of Speir (1982) and more recently Silverman, Baker and Keogh (1998), for example, does address the linguistic strategies drawn on by children in defining the terms of routine engagements with adults. Yet the general trend has been to focus on the world of play, where ethnographic approaches, which concentrate on peer relations, have sought to treat children as active participants within their social worlds. James, Jenks and Prout (1998, pp. 195–219), in their recent theoretical text, introduce the notion of the 'tribal child', a conception of the child drawn on by ethnographers which suggests that children perform more effectively as social agents when they are separated from the adult world. The Opies (1969), for instance, in their ethnography of children's games see separation as a virtue in that, left to their own devices, children are able to perform complex social tasks.

An alternative and less relativist approach argues for agency as the full social recognition of children in structural terms. The emphasis on the permanency of childhood, that is, as a feature of all societies, takes us close to the essentialism which features so strongly within the crisis approach. Yet, as I mentioned earlier, the structural approach has an important political dimension in that childhood here is understood as a key feature of the social stratification system in much the same way as 'gender', 'ethnicity' and 'class'. In these terms sociologists are less likely to neglect the position of children. They are more likely to analyse the children's social relations with reference to theories of social inequality and power. A structural approach would see agency as the full social recognition of children. In other words, children need to be accepted as social actors on the same terms as adults. There is an important transformative dimension to agency here. Full social recognition for children requires quite radical changes to the social structure.

The notion of invisibility makes it difficult to think of children as social agents. Sociological research has in the main seen children as passive recipients of what parents and teachers do to them in the manner of socialization and education. Despite this, research is starting to identify the influence that children have in a number of different contexts. This influence takes two forms. First, children can be viewed as contesting their subordinate role within family. Cahill's (1990) observations of adults and children in public places can be used to refute the crisis thesis, since he contends that parents still maintain the upper hand when controlling their children, At the same time there is an emphasis here on the contested nature of adult–child relations which moves us away from a 'passive' view of children and a more dynamic theory of socialization. A second approach, exemplified by O'Brien (1995) and Morrow (1996), focuses on the different ways in which children contribute to the family economy. I referred earlier to the work of Alanen (1998), which, apart from attempting to see children as key agents of contemporary change, draws on what she calls 'top-down' and 'bottom-up' methodologies in identifying the ways in which children are both positioned by the constraints of family and social structure and at the same time create spaces within these structures that cannot always be anticipated from above. In Britain the Economic and Social Research Council, the largest social science research agency, is currently funding several projects that are investigating the social worlds of children and their involvement within 'adult' settings (Children 5–16 Research Programme, ESRC, United Kingdom). Although this is a multi-disciplinary initiative, the research teams involved all work from the basic principles of the new sociology of childhood: that the recognition of children's involvement within the research process is a first step towards tackling the structural invisibility of childhood; that children's social competencies are recognized within a variety of social contexts; and that the analyses of children's actions *in situ* suggest that childhood is principally a cultural phenomenon.

Conclusion

As far as the reconstruction of childhood is concerned I have identified two possibilities: the capacity to examine the hidden involvement of children within a range of social settings that are normally seen as the preserve of adults, and a set of conceptual tools that locate children within broader theories of social change. I have argued that the former is now well established through the new sociology of childhood through work that revolves around the subjective realms of children. With respect to the latter, the new sociology of childhood has tapped into a rich vein of theorizing which focuses on the political and cultural position of children, and advances the notion that children need to be accepted as social actors located within the broad parameters of social change. However, this last point has not been accepted within substantive sociological theory. Theories of post- or late modernity have so far signally failed to acknowledge the position of children within the social structure.

We might see the integration of these two themes in terms of the timing of this new sociology of childhood. Sociological theorizing which attempts to make sense of seemingly chaotic social trends in the late twentieth century offers the possibility for 'sub-disciplines' to re-examine their conceptual and methodological infrastructures. Theories of late modernity promote the idea of reflexivity at the everyday level of social action and through the paradigmatic shifts within the social sciences (Giddens, 1991). The effects of the latter are felt within sub-disciplines such as sociology of the family and developmental psychology. In this case family sociologists and psychologists reflect on the status of their data, their subjects and their research techniques through a reappraisal of the concept of socialization. Children who were either ignored or come into view as 'necessarily' and 'naturally' incompetent are now seen in more contested terms as both socially exploited and phenomenologically agentic. Whilst these two positions reveal an important and fruitful theoretical tension within the new sociology of childhood, the idea of childhood as a cultural, political and social configuration is taken as read. Shamgar-Handelman reaffirms this point:

> [C]hildhood is a social invention, no matter what form it may take, so that claims of 'the erosion of childhood' (Suransky, 1982) or of the liquidation of childhood (Hengst, 1987) or the need to 'escape from childhood', its boundaries or determinants, have aroused the disapproval of one or other observer.
>
> (Cited in Asquith, 1996, p. 103)

As such it clearly breaches the assumptions built into the crisis thesis, that demands are made on parents to bring their relationships with their children in line with their children's biological inferiority. The precocious child, the child criminal, the teenage mother are attempts at naming social phenomena that are exceptional or deviant cases. They do not fit within the norm of the nuclear family. They are children who do not conform to the 'facts' of childhood.

In Britain and North America childhood is presenting us with something of a paradox. We can assert the social and political invisibility of children and their incorporation within categories such as family and household. At the same time we have to acknowledge the centrality of the child and all things 'childish' within the political and social spheres. I will pursue this in later chapters. Suffice to say at this stage that, apart from one or two notable exceptions, the trend towards protectionism and control has produced an inverse relationship: the more we talk about children, the less likely children themselves seem to be part of these dialogues. It is to these dialogues that I turn to in the following chapters.

2 Social Policy and Moral Ambiguity

Introduction

In the previous chapter I argued for childhood as a contested terrain. Sociological theories of childhood disappearance and crisis are reframed in terms of change and social flux. Whilst the trends are still towards strengthening the subordinate roles of children, there is now some recognition that children are socially competent actors. There is thus a degree of ambiguity in the way that we view children. In this chapter I focus more on the way that childhood is viewed within the policy domain. In particular, I examine the kinds of ideas on childhood to develop from recent child-care and education policy. Theories of crisis draw on policy as a means of moral rescue. The state is drawn on in 'freeing' families and repositioning children. I will advance the notion that moral ambiguity rather than moral rescue is a key theme running through recent child policy.

In later chapters I refer to other policy realms. My reasons for focusing on child care and education here are twofold. First, both policy realms correspond to the two key sites inhabited by children in developed countries: the 'home' and the school.[1] Second, in the last decade or so reform within both educational and child-care spheres has radically altered the professional and political landscapes for those working with children. We need to assess these changes in terms of the possibilities they offer for altering social relations within and between these spheres. We also need to assess the broader impact of these changes for adult–child relations.

In the first part of this chapter I outline the 'crisis' thesis with reference to the relationship between family and state. In particular, I examine the somewhat puzzling role that the state plays in the 'moral rescue' of childhood. This is followed in the second part by a reappraisal of state action and policy in terms of what Asquith (1996, p. 104) calls a dialectical relationship between childhood/family and state. I go on to analyse child policy with reference to the notion of moral ambiguity. In particular, I point to three key dimensions which complicate our ways of viewing children: the restructuring of parents' relations with their children and the state with reference to the notion of parental responsibility; the repositioning of child workers with regard to the idea of professional accountability; and within a child-care context, the repositioning of children as social agents.

Policy as Moral Rescue

In the last chapter I assessed the 'crisis of childhood' thesis in terms of the alleged decline of 'the family'. Ideas of precocity and disorder which are used to characterize the absence of the child are linked to problems that adults face in asserting their authority over children within families. If we assess this in terms of the broader policy issues of care, control and education, the role of the state becomes a key reference point for theories that link children and family to the social and political structure. Pursuing the theme of childhood in crisis, the argument has tended to counterpoise the 'collectivist' state with the 'individual' parent or family.[2] In their analysis of the role of the social services Dingwall et al. set out this opposition.

> They [the social services] cannot be given the legal power to underwrite an investigative form of surveillance without destroying the liberal family. At the same time, the state cannot opt out. There is a collective interest in the moral and physical wellbeing of future citizens, in the quality of social reproduction . . .
>
> (1995, p. 220)

A perennial issue when the relationship between the state and family is being theorized is finding some sort of balance between the rights that children have to 'provision' and 'protection', which are defined by the state, and maintaining the integrity of the private nuclear family as expressed through the interests that parents have in their children. As far as the crisis theorists are concerned, it is these parental interests that take precedence over any abstract and institutionally structured notions of children's welfare and needs. The latter, in effect, are seen as ideological devices which support the intrusion of a whole range of welfare state agencies into family life. Within this frame of reference the idea of children's welfare, like the current fashion for children's rights, can always be invoked by those who seek to conceal their own collective professional interests in and against the common and preferential practices of parents.

With respect to the social position of children, the family in its 'untouched' form is seen to provide the grounds for securing the integrity of the idea of childhood because relations stabilize at a point where parents are said to have authority over their children, where there are clear generational boundaries between parents and their children (Lasch, 1977; Popenoe, 1988; Murray, 1989). This recentring of parents, which in the process reinforces the idea of the ownership of children, is based on an idealized model of family life. First of all, the family is seen to be a natural and timeless institution. Family relations are supposedly grounded in biology, which shapes an instinctive need for both mothers and fathers to protect and nurture their children. Second, for some traditionalists the issue is not simply returning to generational divisions but also reasserting a 'natural' sexual division between mother and father. As I argued in the previous chapter, the problem of children being 'out of place' is linked to an absence of appropriate gender role models. In these terms the single-parent family will not do, for the simple reason that the generational boundary can only be sustained if there exist both male and female adult role models.

Third, child care is argued to be most appropriately and effectively executed within the nuclear family where parents have a degree of privacy and autonomy. Left to their own devices, parents are said to be best placed to provide children with appropriate moral character and support. Any movement from the outside into this private realm is argued to have a deleterious effect on the child's development, as well as undermining the sense of moral responsibility that parenthood is supposed to bestow on adults. Thus the private and autonomous family aids the socialization of the child but it also importantly clarifies the roles that parents play as socializers-in-chief. A fourth feature follows: the family is the primary source of moral and emotional support for children. This means that family comes first in the sense that, for most children, parents are the initial point of contact with the social world. Parents are also primary in that they are seen to be the most formative influence over children, particularly in their early years. In his review of neo-conservative views on the family, Roche (1992, p. 94) indicates that a recurring theme is that 'the family incubates citizen potential; it incubates people capable of becoming citizens and of acting like this in the public sphere'. Family, and in particular parents, mediate between the asocial child and the wider society. The socialization paradigm is discussed in the following chapter in more detail. We need only note here that most professional and lay practices relating to child care and education are driven by assumptions built into this paradigm that suggest that what parents do to children in the first few years of their lives has far-reaching consequences for both children and, arguably, parents themselves.

If we characterize the political culture in Britain since the late nineteenth century in terms of welfare-state building, then the crisis thesis model of state–family relations is irrevocably conflictual. Historically speaking, this tension has been characterized as a shift from *laissez-faire* thinking in Britain in the late nineteenth century – an emphasis on parental autonomy and rights and a residual role for the state – to a position in the latter half of the twentieth century where the state takes a more active role in child care (Fox-Harding, 1991). The story goes that, from some notional high point around the late nineteenth century, sexual and generational divisions within the nuclear family were progressively blurred as welfare capitalism eroded the private realm of family life. Christopher Lasch (1977), in his critique of the state, refers to the work of Ellen Richards, a key figure in the development of modern social work, arguing that the professional establishment in the United States distrusts the 'natural' capacities of parents to take care of their children. Citing Richards, 'If the State is to have good citizens . . . we must begin to teach the children in our schools, and begin at once, that which we see they are no longer learning in the home' (1977, p. 14). Social workers, teachers and marriage counsellors were to take over the role of 'parent' by assuming socialization responsibilities. A conflictual relationship between family and state exists because child-rearing roles cannot be assumed by state agencies for the mystical 'union of love and discipline' can only be transmitted to children by biological parents, those charged with the responsibility for setting clear boundaries between an increasingly hostile outside world and family as sanctuary (Lasch, 1977, p. 3). There is an element of romanticism here, the evocation of a golden past where roles and identities within the family in its natural and unsullied form were naturally ordered, where this ordering insulated individuals from the 'external' rigours of industrialization.

In terms of the reassertion of 'childhood' these historical and political processes need to be reversed – families and, by implication, children are to be 'freed' from state control. Yet this is a very limited form of freedom. Family here is addressed as if it resembled the individual, what Morgan (1985, p. 111) terms 'methodological familism'. In political terms 'the family' takes on the same characteristics as the individual, a solid easily identifiable entity that can be held up as a natural unit against which the artificial disposition of the state is measured. If we disaggregate this individual unit, what is really being freed is that which is taken to be natural *within* the nuclear family, in particular the labour of fathers – the reassertion of 'economic man' and the authority that parents have over children. Furthermore, this freedom is granted at the expense of others within the family.[3]

How is this freedom to be restored? Various authors have referred to a seemingly inconsistent idea that the state is used to free individuals and families from state intervention. Polanyi (1957), in his classic historical account of nineteenth-century political economy, argues that market systems and state intervention have never been mutually exclusive. The state is frequently drawn on in developing market structures and given that, historically speaking, societies never reach a perfect state of *laissez-faire*, the state becomes a precondition of economic liberalism. There is clearly a parallel to be drawn between the pursuit of economic liberty in the nineteenth century and Stuart Hall's (1983) characterization of the political culture in Britain and North America in 1970s and 1980s in terms of the 'free market, strong state'. In the modern period a whole raft of legislation has been passed that has privatized and deregulated local and national state involvement within the economic realm. The moral case was put for this attack on 'collective' interests as a consequence of the way we are supposed to gravitate naturally towards expanding our individual freedoms. Intervention in the pursuit of 'individual freedom' is seen by some as a form of moral rescue whereby families, individuals and, by implication, children are repositioned within some natural moral order through political changes designed to remove the influence of the state.

If we refer back to the earlier discussion on the underclass, the problem is perceived not so much to be an absence of freedom *per se*, but a rootless amoral freedom which loosens the ties that bind children to their biological parents. One solution seems to be to invoke the notion of economic man: to force men back into the labour market by restricting their access to welfare, thereby compelling them to become self-sufficient economically (Gilder, 1982). Through the disciplines of the workplace and cultural notions attributed to the idea of work, men are supposed to become morally responsible in behaviour and lifestyle and in their commitments to other members of their families. At the same time welfare is restricted in order to make it more difficult for young women to reject marriage and their own families of origin by becoming pregnant and relying on state support. What Murray (cited in Roche, 1992, p. 101) calls the 'natural' inclinations of young women to bear and rear children have to be restricted in the interests of social and moral order. Introducing policies to limit welfare is supposed to provide a moral rationale for the recentring of the nuclear family. Economic independence generates traditional commitments to socialization and, importantly from this viewpoint, reasserts parental authority. In these terms freedom is expanded at the economic level as a means of restricting personal freedoms at the moral and social levels for those felt to be dependants of economic man.

Child Policy and Moral Ambiguity

What I am hinting at here is that proponents of childhood in its unreconstructed form have a rather inconsistent view of social policy and, by implication, the role of the state. 'Policy' is here seen as the way that state action undercuts the structural position of children. By this I mean that children are less childlike because the ties that bind them to their subordinate position, the relations they have with their biological parents, have been loosened through the actions of external agencies of child support. At the same time policy might be utilized in freeing the institution of childhood by reaffirming the importance of the nuclear family. The state is involved in making families more self-sufficient. Freed from the intrusions of welfare supports, common sense, tradition and instinct exert a gravitational force on parents' abilities to reaffirm their authority over their children. The state, by the strengthening of the autonomous family, rescues the institution of childhood. Of course, this has quite opposite effects for parents and children, with the former's position being strengthened at the expense of the latter. The notion of individual freedom has quite different consequences for children and adults. I will deal with this tension later in the substantive discussion of child policy. The point here is that policy cannot be simply activated by interested parties in the defence of individual freedoms and at the same time form the basis of a critique of state activities because it denies individual freedoms.

Although there is no attempt to deny the salience, not to say the heuristic qualities of a conceptual framework which differentiates public and private realms, we need to move beyond any naturalized relationship between family/childhood and policy/state. I want to propose that family and by implication childhood, at least the modern western version, are intimately connected in historical and theoretical terms with social policy developments. Social policy cannot simply be seen to be outside the institution of family. The same might be said about the relationship between the idea of childhood and the institutions that are set up to protect, nurture and develop children (Asquith, 1996). From a British vantage point, Rose (1992) and Hendrick (1997) refer, among other things, to the way that the state from about the late nineteenth century onwards promoted the idea of the nuclear family and thus underwrote a dominant conception of childhood as characterized by protection and vulnerability. From a French perspective, the work of Donzelot (1979) and Aries (1961) identifies respectively the importance of schooling and public and voluntary welfare agencies in the shaping of modern views on French families and childhood. Donzelot's work in particular is instructive here. He outlines the way in which public and voluntary welfare throughout the nineteenth and most of the twentieth centuries has been concerned with how to bind parents to the state without the necessity of intervention or family break-up. The convergence of a series of quite disparate historical factors, among others the economic cost to the state of collective child care and the development of welfare professions which drew on psychoanalytic techniques of support, restricted state activity to policing the perimeters of family life. Through this policing, Donzelot argues, the state eventually comes to maintain the integrity of the boundary between itself and the responsibilities that parents have. It would be inappropriate to think of social policy as a form of moral rescue. Donzelot's argument directly confronts the 'crisis of childhood' thesis. There is no *a priori* family as such, to liberate from the clutches of rapacious state bureaucrats and professionals. Neither, for that matter, can the state be used to rescue the moral integrity of family. Through what Donzelot calls 'the social', state agencies and families are locked into a series of mutually binding relationships such that one cannot exist without the other.

We need not go this far in rejecting completely any essential notion of family or childhood. I merely want to draw attention to the possibility that changes in institutions dealing with children might follow a similar pattern with respect to any changes in our understanding of childhood. Jumping ahead of the analysis of policy, we might reinterpret the 'crisis of childhood' in terms of the morally ambiguous position of children, which reflects the ambiguous role that child workers play in supporting children and their families (see Hendrick, 1997). I shall argue that there is no clear-cut policy agenda with regard to the relations between parents, their children and institutions with an interest in childhood. Policy, if anything, serves to confound these relationships and produce moral ambiguity. The basic thrust of this chapter is that recent child policy offers few consistent and unambiguous guidelines as to the way children are to be treated by adults. I shall illustrate this moral ambiguity with reference to a common theme within child-care and educational policy contexts, the idea of parental responsibility.

Within both child-care and educational contexts parents are targeted in terms of ideas that define their responsibilities towards their children. Yet a reading of the legislation concerning probable effects on interested parties and in relation to the broader cultural context suggests that parental responsibility can be defined in three distinct if not mutually exclusive ways.[4] In the first case there is a presumption that the parent rather than the state takes on the role of caretaker of children (Archard, 1993, p. 52). This is based on three factors: that children are vulnerable and socially incompetent and need to rely on adult protection and guidance; that parents are adults and therefore competent, with the ability to make rational autonomous decisions; and finally that parents have a special relationship with their children. Thus, left to their own devices, parents know best how to take care of their children (Goldstein, Freud and Solnit, 1980). Responsibility here incorporates a strong element of powers or rights. These powers are exercised within the private autonomous institution of family. The parent speaks on behalf of the child; has the authority to moralize, control and discipline as well as providing for his or her material well-being. In this sense we can say that the parent has ownership of the child. We can talk here of *responsibilities as rights*.

A second way of viewing parental responsibility is to emphasize the moral basis to this idea that parents 'own' children. There is no attempt to deny here the special rights that parents have *vis-à-vis* the state in relation to child care, and there is, importantly, no attempt to reject the notion of children as immature and incompetent. But the focus is on how these parental responsibilities are discharged as moral obligations. Responsibilities here are more publicly defined obligations or duties. 'Ownership' of children here, if we can talk in these terms, has a collective ring to it. There is still an emphasis on the individual, but an individualism linked to the role that parents play as moral and social guarantors of children's futures. We can talk here of *responsibilities as obligations*. Rather than emphasize the rights parents have, the concern here is on how social, political and legal expectations structure the notion that parents have to do certain things for their children. A third form of parental responsibility revolves around the notion of the 'responsible parent', a rhetorical device for signalling that a range of social problems have their origins within the home. This conception points to a set of social scientific, professional and lay theories of social breakdown. Parents are blameworthy; parents are held responsible in the sense that they have inadequately socialized their children. Thus social problems such as delinquency, lack of school achievement and emotional retardation are said to be caused by something that parents did or did not do to their children. In this third way we have *responsibility as blame*. There is some overlap between the second and third models. The blaming notion presupposes that parents are morally obliged and expected to take responsibility for the children's wrongdoings. But whereas the obligations model would not necessarily hold the parental causally responsible – the origins of the child's problems may not lie in the nature and quality of parent–child relations – the imputation of blame suggests that parents are responsible in the sense that their action or inaction has created the situation whereby they are to be held responsible.[5]

Through an examination of the 1989 Children Act and recent education reform I want to propose that there are elements of all three forms of parental responsibility. What we have here is a series of potentially quite dramatic shifts in thinking around the relations between children, parents and child workers. At the same time there is no clear sense in which these relationships are being strengthened because of the potentially competing interests held by the three parties. I will argue that this is due in part to the ambiguous way that the concept of parental responsibility is applied within these two policy fields. Policy thus reinforces the broad thrust of chapter 1 that boundaries, positions and conceptions of childhood are now more contested. I return to this point in the concluding section.

1989 Children Act

Given the political context of demands for a more minimalist welfare state and more cost-effective local government, the 1989 Children Act which covers England and Wales seems quite a radical piece of legislation. One of the key aims of the Act is to ensure that the needs and welfare of children are met by professionals, parents and in some cases children themselves. When we bear in mind the all-embracing nature of the notion of 'welfare', the implications of the Act are potentially quite costly in meeting the various demands of a child's welfare. Another key aim of the Act is to attempt to clarify the respective claims on children made by parents and child workers. If we return to the quotation from Dingwall et al. (1995) cited earlier, the Act is attempting to balance the interests of parents and welfare professionals. The implications for the positions of parents, child workers and children are far from clear. My contention is that this lack of clarity is a product of the way that the concept of parental responsibility is ambiguously applied within the Act. The Children Act opens with a statement on the parent–child relationship. Parents' responsibilities are defined as 'all the rights, duties, power, responsibilities and authority which by law a parent of a child has in relation to the child and his property' (Part I, section 3). This definition is not particularly helpful in that it includes elements of 'rights' and obligations ('duties'). Freeman refers to the fragility of the Act in that it may

simply be glossing over fundamental historical tensions mentioned earlier between the individual and particular interests of parents and the
collective interests of the state, what he calls 'reconciling the irreconcil-
able' (1992, p. 5).

Parton (1996) argues that although there has been a progressive shift
towards more state involvement in child-care matters, it is the interpretation of these trends that count. Until the 1970s, the social services was
seen as a supportive prop for families in trouble, whereas more recent
political concern has been expressed that suggests a conflictual relationship between state and family which I referred to earlier in terms of a
neo-conservative critique of the welfare state. Other interpretations hold
that the Act is more substantial in that it comes down on one side rather
than the other. John Eekelaar (1991) and Michael Freeman (1992) argue
that the definition and thrust of the Act is a precursor to a much stronger
emphasis on parents' rights rather than obligations. In these terms the
1989 Act reverses earlier 'interventionist' legislation like the 1975
Children Act which extended the coercive powers of the state in making
it easier for local authorities to transfer children at risk from the birth
home to a foster home. It does this by bringing concepts like family privacy and autonomy into the foreground. According to Eekalaar (1991)
parenthood is reordered as a natural state set against institutional character of agencies sponsored by the state. The Act seems to draw on
Dingwall et al.'s (1995) notion of the rule of optimism in asserting that
there is a presumption in favour of the parent where the case has to be
made by the state for a care order separating children from their parents.
Prevailing theory, custom and practice here locate children within the
family, their allegedly natural environment, and thus parents are
expected to act beneficently towards their children unless there is strong
evidence to the contrary, as Fox-Harding (1991, p. 185) argues in her
review of the Act, 'the order [state intervention] must positively contribute to the child's welfare. This principle seeks to keep compulsory
intervention to a minimum in both private and public child care law and
to reinforce rather then undermine parental responsibility.'
Responsibility here is defined in terms of parents' rights.

An alternative interpretation rests on the idea that responsibilities
are more clearly defined in relation to obligations parents have towards
their children which are closely monitored by the state (Fox-Harding,
1991). In one sense obligations are concomitants of rights. The obligations that parents have towards their children presuppose that parents
have the resources and autonomy within which they can discharge their
responsibilities appropriately and efficiently. In theory, parents have
obligations because they have rights denied to other socializing agencies.

Although responsibilities suggest both powers and duties, it is significant that the Act starts with questions of obligations. This is because the notion of duties is consonant with the key principle of the Act – the need to secure the welfare of the child. The reference point here is not the integrity of the family or the proprietorial interests of parents but the needs and welfare of the child. As is clearly stated in the Act, the child's welfare is paramount.

What we have here is a movement away from parents and by implication family in favour of a set of minimum requirements underwriting the child's well-being. We can go back to the presumption in favour of parents. Although the Act might make it more difficult for cases to be brought before the court, the case for intervention can be more easily made. Previously, in making a case social workers relied on evidence of damage or abuse that had already taken place. Social workers can now make a case for a placement of safety order on the basis of 'likely significant harm': perceived rather than actual harm. Professional judgements, in theory, come into play here in defining more precisely what the child's welfare means and in assessing the future orientation of the parent–child relationship. This interpretation suggests that pressures can be brought to bear on parents if they do not discharge their responsibilities as obligations. Furthermore, as Freeman succinctly states, 'parental responsibility . . . is never lost by parents, even where it may seem they have behaved without it' (1992, p. 4). Parents maintain their ties with their children and by implication some notion of ownership in situations where their children have been taken into care. In one sense we may be identifying a rights approach in that children are organically tied to their parents. But clearly these are circumstances where parents' obligations are spelled out, where there is little semblance of family autonomy, where parents' moral positions as caretakers are under close scrutiny.

A final interpretation offered by Parton (1996) is that the Act in principle offers a framework for professionals and parents to work together. 'Partnership' is the buzzword here rather than surveillance or scrutiny. Parents, children and professionals work together in defining the specifics of 'responsibility' through negotiated plans, through an emphasis on the state underwriting the parents' responsibilities and through a more inclusive notion of children's welfare and needs. According to this interpretation there are elements of rights and obligations here. In sum: there is little agreement on how to view the Act with reference to the positions of children, parents and professionals. We cannot read off from the Children Act either the reassertion or the resignation of childhood. What we can say at this point is that the state through the Children Act generates rights and obligations. In particular, models of the 'good' or 'responsible' parent can be read off from policy that has an influence and importance well beyond the minority of families directly affected by the Act.

Education Reform and the Responsible Parent

The Children Act reveals the problems that researchers and policy makers have in balancing 'individual' and 'collective' interests in children. The Act produces moral ambiguity in setting out parent–state relations for it implies that parents are both empowered and constrained, privileged and pressurized. The same can be said within an educational context. Educational policy offers conflicting accounts of the position of parents, emphasizing both rights and obligations with arguably a more recent shift towards the notion of parents as culpable agents. The agenda in the 1970s and 1980s prioritized the empowering of parents through a market-oriented model of education. Several English-speaking countries during the 1980s were working from a privatizing economic agenda capitalizing on a variety of public concerns over both the alleged failure of state education to service the economy and provide children with a moral and social framework of 'standards'.[6]

In Britain the 1986 and 1988 Education Acts can be seen as attempts to fragment the collective interests of local government, educational authorities and the teaching profession through the introduction of market principles such as competition, choice and accountability (Ball, 1994; Walford, 1996). In the process education reform was attempting to restructure relations between 'individuals' and the state by redesignating the rights that parents have over the school in relation to their children's education. Recent research suggests that some groups of parents are both unable and unwilling to take up these new powers offered by government (Hughes, Nash and Wikeley, 1994). Nevertheless, the parent as consumer has become a compelling reference point for the provision of education. As Ball (1994, pp. 65–66) argues, there is now a 'new culture of schooling, a culture of commodification and output indicators which articulates with the culture of choice and relative advantage into which parents are being drawn'. First of all, legislation lifts restrictions on school enrolment and opens up the possibilities for parents to send their children to schools outside their local catchment areas. School choice is enhanced in the way that schools are compelled to provide parents with more information. The Parent's Charter, distributed to all households in 1991, encourages parents to make claims on the school in providing a wide range of information from summaries of inspection reports to details of the school's arrangements for sex education

(Department for Education, 1991). Parents are thus supposed to be in a stronger position to make informed choices on where to send their children. Second, the 1988 Act allows schools to opt out of local education authority control and become grant-maintained. This gives schools greater autonomy from the local state, with funding coming direct from central government. Parents as consumers are the arbiters of this move in that the decision to opt out is based on the outcome of a vote by the parents of children at the school.

It can also be said that education reform affects relations between parents and children in the sense that parents' powers as socializers have been enhanced. The introduction of a more competitive ethic in education allied to the demands of the national curriculum potentially strengthen the primary position of the parent in the socializing process in two ways. First, the emphasis on academic achievement through the national curriculum and the need to quantify and compare this achievement potentially weakens any pastoral ('welfarist') expertise that a school might have in dealing with difficult children (Wyness, 1996, pp. 141–143). The notion of supporting pupils through counselling and through more discursive settings such as personal and social education becomes more difficult to sustain as teachers spend proportionately more of their time responding to the didactic demands of the national curriculum. As teachers become stretched in their more conventional teaching roles in class, the wider social context of the child's family and community recedes from the teacher's purview. The role of the teacher *in loco parentis* is thus more difficult to sustain.

Allied to this, recent well-publicized criticisms of teaching styles may have the effect of shifting teachers' practice away from targeting the individual child and working from assumptions about his or her emotional and family background to a more traditional and formal class-based approach (Alexander, Rose and Woodhead, 1992). Recent education reform and thinking around pedagogy, particularly in primary schools, may strengthen the idea that child development is not the province of the schoolteacher, but is something that primarily takes place within the home. Moreover, the notion of child-centredness is also linked to a form of progressivism whereby teachers are supposed to relate to children in less hierarchical ways. The encouragement of a teaching ethos which reasserts the sovereign authority figure of the teacher and an emphasis on a centrally administered curriculum potentially reverses this form of child-centredness in that it brings teacher-centred interests dominated by the curriculum rather than 'familial matters' in line with the authority of parents as primary socializers. Children are thus encouraged to relate to parents and teachers as authority figures with their own respective spheres of influence, with the parent as ultimate arbiter of the child's well-being. Thus we can say that the idea of education as a quasi-market with the concomitant notion of the parent as consumer strengthens the rights version of parental responsibility. Parents are expected to know what their children's educational needs are and are to be free to express these rights within an education market-place. It must be stated here that the introduction of the national curriculum undercuts the individualizing tendencies of open enrolment and 'opting out'. I will not dwell on the contradiction between parents' ability to choose the form of their children's schooling but not the content, for this has been discussed elsewhere (Hargreaves and Reynolds, 1990). However, the centralizing tendencies of the national curriculum force teachers into more restricted pedagogic positions which indirectly reaffirms the parents' socializing powers. A by-product of a centralized curriculum and teaching ethic is the strengthening of parents' responsibilities as rights.

In another sense, some of the unintended as well as intended consequences of education reform would seem to be implying the 'obligations' and 'blaming' models of responsibility. Despite the intentions of policy makers to redress the balance of power between parents and schools through the notion of parent power, we can refer to the way that parental choice as a means of asserting a parent's rights has been superseded by a process of schools selecting pupils potentially on the basis of 'parental criteria'. First of all, the imposition of a market framework leads to the better or 'magnet' schools becoming oversubscribed. This means that in a *de facto* sense these schools are able to select their intake of pupils. The notion of opening up education to the market-place also has the potential to lead to a range of social and public order problems which again place parents on the defensive. Schools competing for scarce resources have the ability not only to restrict the entrance of children with 'irresponsible parents', they are in a position to exclude pupils who are perceived to be compromising a school's position within the market-place (Carlen, Gleeson and Wardhaugh, 1992). Alongside the truant, the excluded pupil gets caught up in a web of public associations between the absent pupil and the nascent delinquent which puts more pressure on parents to discharge their responsibilities as obligations. Whether formally or informally, schools may be in a position to choose children of 'responsible' parents as pupils. Second, there has been a change in the rules, with schools now able to select a proportion of their pupils on ostensibly academic grounds (*The Times*, 24 November 1995, p. 1). Yet, given that there are increasing problems of aggression in schools, and given that schools are in the business of marketing themselves in terms of relative pupil success, it would be easy to see 'familial' criteria becoming a prominent means of distinguishing between potentially good and potentially bad pupils.[7] Parents as consumers are in the ironic position of having to present themselves to prospective schools as very 'responsible' agents. Given the concerns that head teachers might have over their schools' positions in a localized education market-place, we might be coming close to parental responsibility in its third form, as part of a culture of blame.[8] The focus on pupil output in both intellectual and behavioural terms may mean that judgements on the future conduct of a school's pupil intake may be based on the evaluation of parents as consumers along a spectrum of blameworthiness.

The current British Labour government is more explicit in questioning the moral basis to parents' ownership of the education process. In part this is linked to the demand for parents to become more involved in their children's academic development. All sorts of initiatives are currently being developed nationwide to encourage parents to take more responsibility for, among other things, monitoring their children's homework and spending more time with them reading. But this trend towards encouraging greater involvement is also linked to broader 'social' factors referred to earlier which link the school with the local community. A series of isolated violent disturbances inside and around the perimeters of British schools, public concerns over truancy and school exclusion and a general anxiety over a perceived decline in standards of school behaviour have exercised educational minds on the problems of responsibility in behavioural, as well as educational, terms. The Labour government's White Paper, *Excellence in Schools* (1997), refers to the 'responsibilities as rights' theme in setting out what schools can do for parents in areas such as parental access – the paper aims to improve the clarity of information provided by schools for parents. It also refers to an increase in the representation of parents on governing bodies. But there now also seems to be a shift towards what parents can do for schools. The document encourages 'parents and local communities [to be more] effectively involved in the education of children' (p. 13). Some authors hint at the idea of responsibility as obligations being softened through the rhetoric of home–school partnerships (Vincent and Tomlinson, 1997). What we can say here is that parents become more incorporated in the broader project of educating children. Parents are expected to get more involved in supporting their children's classroom work. More significantly, the language of partnership is supplemented by talk of a home–school contract. This hinges on parents delivering what Sharp and Green (1975, p. 86) call the 'school trained child'. In effect, home–school contracts become ways of pinning down allegedly errant parents by prescribing their responsibilities to the school for, among

other things, their children's school attendance, behaviour and homework (pp. 54–55).

Culture of Blame

There is little consensus over how the Children Act repositions parents
and professionals because the concept of parental responsibility is morally
ambiguous. It connotes family autonomy and the ongoing policing of
family integrity by the state. There is similarly little consensus on the
location of parental responsibility within education reform. If we place
both policies alongside less family- or child-oriented legislation, we
strengthen the notion of responsibility in its third form as part of a culture of blame. Both sets of policies go along with other notable social
legislation, such as the 1991 Criminal Justice Act, which states that parents are responsible in the sense that they 'pay' for their children's
wrongdoing. Parents not only have to do unspecified things that underwrite their children's 'welfare', but they are supposed to take
responsibility for their children's wrongdoings. In the last two or three
years curfews have been introduced as experiments in towns and cities in
Britain and the United States. These experiments bear down on the
'controlling' abilities of adult members of the community by encouraging parents to keep their children at home after certain specified times in
the evening (Rufford, 1997). The 1998 Crime and Disorder Act directly
and indirectly makes further provisions for parents as responsible agents
and extends the power of the local authorities over children. 'Parenting
Orders' are introduced which require parents of 'delinquent' children to
attend counselling sessions on parenting skills. Because of parents'
imputed inattention or lack of disciplinary skills, they are exposed to
more explicit models of 'good' or 'responsible' parenting. Curfews are
now legislated for, with local authorities having powers to initiate local
curfews. Finally, the Act makes provisions for Child Safety Orders
whereby children under the age of 10 who commit what would normally
be seen as a crime (children under 10 cannot, legally speaking, commit
crime) are placed under the supervision of the local authority for between
3 and 12 months. Parents are both responsible for their children's welfare
and are potentially to blame for their children's behaviour. The connection is pretty clear. Duties are externally defined and measured against
their children's present and future actions.

It is an interesting question as to whether professionals and parents
themselves carry around in their heads what Dingwall et al. (1995) call
lay social theories which centre on the moral blameworthiness of parents.
But there has arguably been a shift towards a culture of blame whereby

moral issues are framed in terms of the actions of parents. The argument addressed earlier on the loss of childhood evokes notions of parental autonomy and privacy which presuppose that parents are, by and large, dealt with according to the rights they have in relation to state agencies. These rights mark out the sacred territory of parenthood. Irrespective of whether families are more or less privatized now, Chris Harris' (1983) work on the problems that parents face in asserting their authority or rights suggests a historical shift in emphasis from the 'inner' capacities of parents to externally defined notions of what parents are expected to do, in effect, the shift from parental authority to parents' responsibilities. I have argued that the concept of responsibility can be interpreted in terms of both rights and obligations. Nevertheless, the thrust of Harris' argument is the same: parents may be more likely to feel causally and morally responsible for their children's perceived shortcomings and told at the same time that they are the primary agents of child care and control (1983, p. 240). Harris spells out the possible implications that the blaming model can have for parents. They are anxious, feel less in control, in many ways unable to grasp precisely what is being asked of them as good or responsible parents.

Although we can go along with Donzelot's (1979) notion of state intervention being conditioned by the search for the self-sufficient family unit, there has been a great deal of movement around, over and upon families from outside with regard to the concept of parental responsibility. As caretakers, as consumers of education and as moral trustees, parents are the agents responsible for the child's welfare. In cultural terms, families exist as a crucial reference point for policy and professional and lay practice. Yet the picture is far from complete. Two key elements are missing: first, the relations that child workers have with each other, their notions of professional accountability; second, the position of children. Both are important because they further complicate relations between child, family and state. I will address each element in turn.

The Accountable Professional

In one important respect professional accountability is built into the concept of parental responsibility. The rights model of responsibilities suggests that parents are responsible because agencies become more accountable in the sense that they are more answerable to parents. This is most clearly expressed through education reform. I referred earlier to the demands on head teachers to supply consumers with a steady flow of information on their schools. Government policy through the Parent's

Charter (1991/1994) gives parents a right to know, to choose, to receive reports, to complain, in general, a right to assess the merits of a particular school with reference to other schools competing within a quasi-market. The disciplinary imperative of the market forces schools to present themselves in all sorts of informal ways to parents.

At the same time there is a compelling 'need to know' what the professionals are doing which is related to, but not directly a result of, market pressures. Howe (1994) drawing on Lyotard's notion of 'performativity', argues that social workers' professional lives are now dominated by rules that govern their performance. The market features as an important reference point in the use of such terms as 'consumer orientation' or 'client-centredness' where 'service delivery' becomes the measurable market commodity. Yet political pressures, 'new managerialist' practices and shifting professional norms are also key factors. In a broader sense, the work of the child professional, both social worker and teacher, is assessed more and more on the basis of quantifiable links between 'inputs' and 'outputs'. Accountability can then be understood as a structural feature of the child worker's practice. Accountability thus becomes an end in itself, part of a general process of rationalizing and commodifing the work of the child professional.

I referred earlier to the political critique of state education with respect to the perceived failings of the curriculum and the teaching profession. From the Black Papers in the late 1960s through to the Hillgate pamphlets of the 1980s teachers have been under considerable political pressure to conform to a more standardized and individualized conception of teaching. This has been aided somewhat by the introduction of the Office for Standards in Education (Ofsted), the new school inspectorate answerable directly to central government (DES, 1992). Ofsted is linked to the market because it is supposed to provide consumers with an official and allegedly impartial evaluation of a school's performance over a predetermined period of time. This supposedly allows consumers to make an informed choice about where to send their children. At the same time there is an important centralizing thrust to inspection as teachers are subject to the rigours of the inspection process which clearly ties their performance to a set of state-defined indicators of teaching quality. Professional accountability is most clearly and visibly illustrated through the public availability of a school's Ofsted inspection report.

A second notion of teacher accountability can be seen through the internal connections that are made between how well children are doing in class and the quality of teaching. Kelly (1994, p. 65), in his critique of the national curriculum, argues that 'a prime purpose, perhaps *the* prime purpose, of assessment in the National Curriculum is teacher appraisal and accountability [author's emphasis]'. Pupil assessment at all four 'key' stages of development provides an important framework through which teachers' 'input' can be measured for it provides clear and explicit indicators of teachers' performance. Accountability is internal in that test scores can be used as criteria for judgements made within schools about the quality of teaching. The national curriculum, through pupil assessment, thus becomes an important disciplinary mechanism for keeping teachers in line. Moreover, the comparative nature of these test results is also supposed to have a disciplinary effect on head teachers. Again, the market appears as a subtle but compelling reference point. Test results form the basis of comparisons between pupils and between teachers; they also form the basis of comparisons between schools through league tables which provide 'informed' data on the quality of teaching and academic leadership. Ultimately, testing is linked to notions of school 'effectiveness' and 'efficiency' which is supposed to tighten up the practitioners' roles within school.

If we turn to child-care professionals, the same external pressures are brought to bear on social work practice and form the basis of internal as well as external systems of accountability (at the same time there is much less emphasis on the market). The Children Act was partly a result of a series of high-profile events which brought into question the way that social workers went about the business of protecting children. The Cleveland and Orkney cases in the 1980s in one sense illustrated the power that professionals had to summarily separate groups of children from their families on the basis of allegations of abuse. Yet, given the problems attributed to the child protection system of 'under-intervention' in the previous 15 years, the problem was not so much an excess of state power, more a lack of clarity in professional practices and an absence of institutional procedures for regulating the way that social workers protected children.

Several authors have referred to the way that internal and external scrutiny dominates the thinking and practice of child-care professionals. Although the Children Act provides a comprehensive system for professional accountability with the child's welfare as the centrepiece, there has been criticism of the way the Act has been interpreted by state agencies. Parton (1996, 1997) and Dingwall, Eekelaar and Murray (1995) focus on the way that professionals apply the Act more or less exclusively in terms of professional accountability. Paraphrasing Dingwall et al., Parton contends that social work practice has shifted from 'taking the *right* decision to taking a *defensible* decision' (1997, p. 13, author's emphases). Drawing on a key phrase within the Children Act, the identification of 'likely significant harm', social workers have transmuted the concepts of needs and welfare into the calculation of probable risk. This leads to the prioritizing of certain 'significant harms' over others according to what is politically and practically expedient. Dingwall et al. locate these tendencies within bureaucratic and complex systems of control which structure the kinds of decisions made by social workers. I will take up this issue in chapter 3 when outlining the legal position of child protection.[9] What I want to stress at this juncture is that, rather than see professional accountability as an effect of a system which is structured by issues such as child welfare and protection, the professional needs of the child worker become 'paramount'.

The Child as an Accountable Agent

In the previous chapter I argued that despite weighty social theorizing on late or post-modernity, there is little that connects social fragmentation to the changing nature of adult–child relations. In this chapter I have dealt with social fragmentation that results in moral ambiguity by focusing on the way that child policy complicates relations between child workers and among child workers and parents (Oldman, 1994). A final crucial factor which complicates these relationships is the position of the child. In chapter 4 I address this theme more substantively when assessing the position of the new 'schooled' child (Hendrick, 1997). In this final section I will argue that with reference to child care, the idea of children as responsible or accountable agents further complicates networks of responsibility.

The 1989 Children Act focuses on the ways that the child's 'welfare' and 'needs' are defined and met both by the state and the family (see p. 39. The paramountcy principle makes the child a central figure in any decisions taken relating to child care. How might we interpret this notion of paramountcy? I want to concentrate here on three scenarios. First, children become more prominent participants in child-care matters and thus are intimately involved in decision-making processes that directly affect their welfare. Adults therefore become more directly accountable to children. The paramountcy principle refers to welfare as the child's interests rather than some concept of 'need' constructed by adults on behalf of children (see Woodhead, 1997). Second, if we think of children as social agents, does it follow that they can be seen to take more responsibility for their own welfare? In other words, following earlier arguments that suggest that responsibility incorporates obligations as well as rights, can we say that children, as well as becoming more powerful, have become more accountable for their actions? A third possibility is that the child's welfare is the discursive terrain over which adults contest the best approaches to child care. Here the paramountcy principle has less to do with the strengthening of the child's voice and more to do with the perennial issue of adult protection and control. These are themes that structure much of the material discussed in the following chapters. In particular, chapter 3 concerns the way that all three scenarios are in conflict when assessing the child protection system and the problem of child sexual abuse. Here I will confine my brief remarks to scenarios 1 and 2.

Much of the criticism of the Act, at least from the children's rights lobby, does not focus on scenario 2 which would seem to follow from scenario 1. Roger Smith's (1991) promotion of a social contract for children spells out the rights for children rather than the concomitant obligations.[10] The primary focus of the rights lobby is the contention that children's rights, at least of the self-determinist variety, are rather limited within the Children Act (see Franklin and Franklin, 1996). However, there are some elements of scenario 1 within the Act. Although the Act may not be a fully blown charter for children, the position of the 'responsible parent' and 'accountable professional' is further complicated by this piece of legislation because of the possibilities for childhood agency. Parents and professionals not only have to contend with popular, professional and legal conceptions of blame and responsibility, they have to accommodate the possibilities of children themselves becoming subjects as well as objects within a network of child welfare. Care and control may not quite be complemented or supplemented by any conception of children's liberation, but the Act does point to the involvement of children in care proceedings. This involvement can be seen in terms of children's rights and in some cases, by implication, their roles as responsible agents, but it is doubtful whether professionals, in practice, can interpret the child's 'needs' and 'welfare' simply within a 'best interests' framework without any consultation with children.

Reference is made within the Act to adults having to 'ascertain the wishes and feelings of children' before decisions are taken which affect their future relations with their parents and siblings (section 8). The Act further expresses this principle in several ways. First, children are now able to contest (a) Emergency Protection Orders (EPO) which are invoked in the immediate removal of children from their homes (s. 44[7]), and (b) medical examinations and interim care orders (s.43[8]). Second, children are in a position now to review their care proceedings through the newly set up system for complaints. They are also expected to be present at case conferences and have their opinions canvassed. Where children are absent from any review, they are to be consulted and made aware of the results of the review (s. 26[2]). Third, the Children

Act strengthens the nearest thing that Britain has to an advocate for the child, the guardian *ad litem*, who represents the child in court cases. Although the first point implies that children take action without the support or consent of significant adults, guardians *ad litem* are to be used more often and their representation is to be made more obligatory than it was in the past (Fox-Harding, 1991, p. 297). The guardian *ad litem* becomes the child's mouthpiece in negotiating his/her interests in legal situations. One of the implications of this is that the guardian can be put in the position of having to contradict the advice given to the child by the solicitor if the child decides that he or she prefers another course of action (King and Young, 1992).

Conclusion

I started this chapter by examining the idea that the institution of child-hood might be resurrected by strengthening the nuclear family. Yet the means to this resurrection is also one of the major sources of its decay – the modern political state and its capacity to generate social change through policy. Parents, the key agents, lose their authority over their children because they cannot compete with the debilitating and totaliz-ing influence of the state. Childhood loses its shape in that children are less likely to be positioned as subordinates within families. At the same time the state is the architect of the moral rescue of childhood. Policies are designed to force parents to be more self-reliant, which by implica-tion reaffirms the social and political contours of childhood. The fact that the state is both the source of, and the partial solution to, the problem of childhood is largely a product of an inflexible and overly dichotomous model of family–state relations. The problem of childhood thus rests on a series of oppositional elements that sets childhood against state. Childhood, a central feature of family life, is conflated with nature and structured by ideas of autonomy and privacy. The state, in particular the modern welfare variety, on the other hand, is part of the external public world and because of its capacity to expand and monopolize is more or less likely to encroach within the private realm.

I shall go on to outline a more interdependent relationship between family and state. The contours of modern childhood and by implication family life are intimately bound up with the way in which the political realm views the position and condition of childhood. Child policy and the policy agenda are complicit in the fragmenting of adult identities and responsibilities towards children. This can be seen as the contesting of control, authority, responsibilities and rights relating to childhood within child care and education. Whereas the 1989 Children Act appears to bring the private realm of family life within the public domain, recent education reform has arguably 'privatized' what we might term the public realm of schooling. Child-care policy generates expectations of standards of care that open family life up to more public scrutiny. Education policy, on the other hand, conceptualizes the role of parents as a bundle of individual rights, which shifts the balance of power away from the educational establishment. Broadly speaking, I am saying that education policy takes us in one direction, whilst child-care policy takes us in the other. Yet there is a degree of complexity here, for the opening up of both realms is more complex and ambiguous.

The idea of moral ambiguity develops out of a lack of clarity in the way adults are supposed to relate to children and, by implication, the way they are supposed to relate to each other. The analysis of recent child policy highlights this ambiguity. First, both child-care and education policy contexts open up family life to public scrutiny and make parents an important reference point for the care and education of children. This ambiguous position is a result of the way in which the concept of parental responsibility can be read from child policy. Parents are targeted as responsible agents, which has the effect of both strengthening and enervating their positions. Parental responsibility implies a set of exter-nally defined obligations that places demands on parent both as primary socializers and as agents with responsibilities for their children's conduct in school. At the same time presumptions of non-intervention and notions of parental choice appear to hand parents a degree of power and autonomy with respect to managing their children's development.

A second complication shifts the focus away from the specifics of what parents can and cannot do to a more general adult level of analysis. In many ways the notion of parental responsibility has its counterpart in the realm of the child worker, the idea of professional accountability. Surveillance and scrutiny is something that the lay population have to contend with more and more now in their dealings with their children. But it is not simply a question of state professionals skirting around or, in cavalier 'child-saving' fashion, intruding within families. Nor is it for that matter a question of them responding to the variegated demands and needs of parents as consumers. Greater professional accountability is not simply an effect of the empowering of parents as consumers. It has both internal and external ramifications whereby child workers are sub-ject to 'need to know' imperatives which generate more defensiveness and calculation within their associated professions.

A final complicating factor brings us to the conventionally silent but increasingly central figures within this network of responsibility and accountability, the children themselves. This further complicates the policy realm and the position of the respective actors. At this point we can make a clear distinction between the two policy realms. In this chapter I have looked specifically at the position of children within the child-care context. Whereas the historical and political neglect of the child's viewpoint is more or less maintained within an education context (and I will discuss this in more detail in chapter 4), there have been some attempts to bring the children themselves into the policy foreground in child care through the Children Act. It remains to be seen whether children can profit from the limited autonomy granted them. The position of children does largely depend on the prevailing social and political climate. Notions of their autonomy and rights here are more likely to be explored in contexts of social and moral security. Within a climate of fear about aggression, crime and abuse with the requisite focus on protection, blame and falling standards, parents, teachers and social workers will tend to act in ways that restrict the time and space children need to express this autonomy.

3 Child Sexual Abuse
Protection, Prevention and Identification

Introduction

The previous chapter focused on the importance of recent child policy as a political and professional framework for transforming adults' roles and responsibilities towards children's welfare, education and needs. If we refer more specifically to child-care considerations, there has been a shift towards taking the child's views into account. Yet the general trend towards networks of adult responsibility and accountability has been largely dominated by the need to protect children. This is largely to do with the way that the 1989 Children Act was foreshadowed by the public, political and academic concern expressed over the sexual abuse of children. The Children Act became the explicit and formal basis for an expanding and complex child protection system which is crucially centred around the problem of abuse. In this chapter I argue that the problem of child sexual abuse has led to a heightened awareness of the boundaries between adults and children. This awareness is reflected in a series of disparate political, legal and professional initiatives and practices which converge on the treatment of children in ontological, moral and political terms. I examine these concerns and the possible implications they have for our understandings of childhood. To begin with, I examine child protection as an organizing principle for the theorizing of abuse and how best to deal with it. There are two themes: the idea of protection and its implications for adult–child relations, and the influence of an associated concept, socialization. I suggest that assumptions built into these two broad concepts underpin policy and professional practice in the field of child abuse. Moreover, through the discussion of protection and socialization I contend that the adult–child boundary has been strengthened.

In the second and third parts I broaden the discussion of policy and the problem of child sexual abuse and examine a series of local and global policy initiatives, developed as a result of political and social demands for a more protective child-care framework in Europe and the United States. I will argue that these demands take two forms: a need to prevent child abuse and a need to identify child abusers. In both cases I will go on to argue that, rather than simply strengthen the idea of the child as a subordinate subject, these demands have opened up possibilities for children themselves to take more control over their lives. We can begin to detect here more contested and less deterministic conceptions of childhood.

A word on sexual abuse: the substance of my chapter deals with the sexual abuse of children: the conceptual underpinnings of child protection, the preventive and legal and psychological ramifications of the problem. Whilst it might seem that the focus on sexual abuse rather than any of the other three forms – emotional, neglect, physical – is driven by its dramatic, some would say sensationalized, nature, my concerns with the prevention and identification of abuse rest on legal and professional approaches which concentrate solely on the sexual form of abuse. That said, many of the assumptions about childhood and the possibilities for children of altering their social relations with adults generated through the discourse on sexual abuse can be applied to the other forms of abuse. The main focus of this book is the contested conceptions of childhood which tend to revolve around the nature of children's social relations with others. It is patently clear from the understanding of child abuse in all its manifestations that it is a relational phenomenon.

Child Protection

In this section I want to start by addressing the problem of child sexual abuse with reference to the general issue of protection. It is quite revealing that within professional and academic circles we rarely talk publicly about the problem in terms of 'child abuse'; we tend to refer to 'child protection' matters. This may be a question of public and professional sensitivity: the idea of protection suggests more romantic humanitarian notions of saving children; 'abuse' has negative connotations. It may also be a matter of thinking more widely: if we refer to the child protection system we are talking about an elaborate network of institutions which are attempting to deal with the various ramifications of child abuse. I think, though, that the fashion for talking about child protection reflects more fundamental assumptions. As a set of institutional practices child protection has now absorbed broader moral and social reference points such as 'care' and 'welfare' in such a way that child protection is often conflated with child welfare and child care. 'Child protection' is also, significantly, an umbrella term that incorporates a range of ideas and assumptions about the nature of relations between children and adults. Fundamentally, it implies that 'care' and 'welfare' are administered and administrated for children by adults. Child protection implies that things are done to and for children. This 'top-down' model derives partly from the dominant image of the vulnerable child. There is a tendency here to think about protection as a 'human' response on the part of the strong to care for the weaker. Children are to be rescued from one set of dangerous circumstances and placed in safer, protected environments.

It is sometimes difficult to question the motives of professionals who claim to be acting in the interests of the child's basic safety, but their actions can often have negative consequences for children. Protection can sometimes lead to children being excluded from the hub of their social relations, in the process reinforcing their already marginal social status. As I shall demonstrate in the following chapter, schooling is a crucial locus of the exclusion and segregation of children. Yet the impetus to rescue children where they are perceived to be in danger, particularly from other members of the family, leads to the exclusion of the child from the few situations that bring him or her into less structured, less regulated contact with others.

For some, child protection becomes little more than a cover for more control and regulation of children. As Mary John puts it in her analysis of children's rights, '"protection" within the family may mean little more than a cover for paternalistic practices that may restrict the child's autonomy and be antithetical to the achievement of rights' (1995, p. 107). That said, the impetus to protect children by means of various forms of safe enclosure can now be mediated through consultation with the children themselves. As I outlined in the previous chapter, the 1989 Children Act encourages professionals to consult with children about securing their welfare. Nevertheless, the emotive and moral tone of child protection, with its connotations of saving the child, implies few alternatives to working with children than the 'top-down' approach. The Children Act offers only limited opportunities to view adult–child relations in more horizontal or equitable terms.

Socialization

A second and associated way of framing the problem of child sexual abuse is through socialization theory. Here we have a more specific, more precise and academically oriented version of protection. Child protection implies a paternalistic and overarching relationship with children, who are assumed to have fewer resources and skills for looking after themselves. Whilst socialization theory provides a much clearer conception of the child's status within the discourse of abuse, at the same time the more subtle and nuanced features of socialization theory conceal its power as a framework for locking the child into a subordinate social position. Socialization has attained almost a paradigmatic status within theory and practice. In part this is due to the way it is interpreted as a scientific endorsement of a relationship which many people take to be natural and biological, the relationship between parent and child. What socialization theory also does is to frame the problem of child sexual abuse in such way that it offers accounts and explanations of abuse and at the same time unwittingly reinforces the possibilities for abuse.

In western liberal societies the process of becoming an adult is synonymous with the development of the 'individual' character or personality. This is taken to be formed in the crucial early phase when the child is most dependent on the adult socializer. Children are expected to develop confidently in safety through their relationships with significant adult others. In particular, both functionalist sociology and developmental psychology – which I take here to be strands of socialization theory – stress the importance of the biological parent and, to a certain extent, the teacher. They become responsible agents in propelling the child towards a state of rationality and morality. The practice of parents, teachers and a range of other socializing agents is heavily imbued with what Prout and James (1997, p. 13) call an 'implicit binarism'. Socializing children involves moving them from an initial state of irrationality and amoralism to a fully developed state of moral and cognitive maturity, to what is commonly taken to be the 'rational individual'. The child's status develops in and through this process of socialization, which is supposed to take place within the socially approved boundaries of the nuclear family.

In the original early state the child is seen to be dependent on the interests and actions of the biological parent. The idea of dependence draws on Bowlby's notion of the child's early physical and emotional attachment to the mother. Bowlby's theory locks the mother into this dependency relationship in that she is biologically driven to provide continuous emotional and physical care for at least the first two years of the child's life. Parsons refers to this attachment or bonding as primary socialization (1965). The significance of primary relations lies in highlighting the importance of the mother and later on the father in making the initial physical and social points of contact with the child. Both Bowlby and Parsons refer to the importance of these early attachments because of the significance they have for the child's subsequent moral and social development. Bowlby famously tried to base his delinquency theory on the absence of early maternal attachments. According to Bowlby, children are more likely to commit crime, more likely to have emotional and psychological problems if there is an absence of continuous physical care in early childhood (reported in Hendrick, 1997). Parsons goes along with the basic thrust of this argument.

> There is reason to believe that, among the learned elements of personality in certain respects the stablest and most enduring are the major value-orientation patterns and there is much evidence that these are 'laid down' in childhood and are not on a large scale subject to drastic alteration during adult life.
>
> [1982, p. 139]

Here we have a clear statement on the 'top-down' nature of socialization. Parents 'lay down' the emotional and cognitive ground rules very early on. This process has potentially serious consequences for children in later life. Thus what parents, particularly mothers, do to their children in the early formative years structures their children's moral and social well-being in later life. As well as concentrating on the mother–child relationship, Parsons also stresses the importance of the father. Through his reworking of Freud's theory he locates the father as an initially shadowy figure in the life of the child who gradually becomes more influential in shaping his or her moral sense of purpose.

Drawing on 'protection' and emotional and physical dependence, Giddens' (1984, pp. 51–60) version of socialization focuses on the idea of trust. Trust is significant because it structures adult expectations about child development as well as forming the basis of the young child's understanding of the social world around the actions of parents. Giddens emphasizes the dynamic relationship between mother and child. He refers to a series of 'developmental' phases – inner conflicts which the child has to master before becoming autonomous; as Giddens puts it, socialization provides for the 'foundation of the capability for a reflexive monitoring of conduct' (ibid., p. 57.)

Whilst the very early period of dependence is characterized by strong physical bonds between child and parents, these bonds are defined in terms of care, nurturing and more basic notions of physical protection. Despite the influence of Freud within socialization theory and his reference to dependence in terms of 'erotic' attachments, there is little sense in which these physical attachments are sexual. Parsons (1954) argues that the proscription of sexual relations between the generations – what is commonly known as the incest taboo – strengthens the integrity of the parents' authority over their children. Socialization theory suggests that strong emotional and physical 'attachments' to both parents abate as the child gradually experiences more of the outside world (Jenks, 1982). In effect, the early attachments wither away as the child moves towards adulthood and independence. What is in the process of being produced here in sociological terms is the independent rational adult; to paraphrase O'Neill (1982, p. 53), in psychological terms the individual becomes the owner of a fully formed 'psyche . . . an enclosed state of consciousness inaccessible to anyone other than its owner'. The binary model referred to earlier is clearly brought out: childhood dependence within a nuclear family setting becomes a precondition of independence and adulthood.

Socialization and Theories of Sexual Abuse

Notions of trust, protection and dependency are ways of describing what has almost become a sacred relationship between parent and child. It is therefore not difficult to see how sexual abuse flagrantly breaches the fundamental tenets of this relationship. It is also not difficult to see how theories of abuse and prescriptions for its treatment rest on altering, breaking and, importantly, renewing this relationship. Furthermore, in maintaining the nuclear family as a biologically and socially essential institution, and by locating children within this private, sacred and emotionally self-sufficient unit which protects and socializes, it is not too difficult to see how the concepts of 'family' and 'parent' are non-negotiable when abuse is being assessed. As La Fontaine puts it when discussing the discourse on abuse, 'parental authority is a matter of rights which are much more often talked about than parental power' (1990, p. 77). Where 'power' might be expressed is within the various explanations of abuse, not as a common feature of all families and adult–child relations, but as a pathological property of abusing individuals, abusing families and abusing classes.

Pathologizing abuse is plainly evident in theories that focus on the predispositions of individual abusers. These take two forms: those theories that focus on the individual traits of abusers, and those that focus on the life experiences of abusers. Saraga (1993), in her review of the child sexual abuse research, refers to the way that professional practice is now more likely to draw on the latter approach. She contends that there are no clear individual 'types' of abusers, nothing biological or psychological that clearly marks one abuser off from another. But there appears to be some sort of professional recognition of the 'life events' approach which focuses on the way adults are more likely to abuse if they have been abused themselves in childhood, what is known as the 'inter-generational transmission of abuse'. This 'cyclical' theory does little more than correlate abusers with the abused. The causal connections are never clearly spelled out. Moreover, a cursory glance at the statistics on the gender profile of abusers and victims would suggest that these correlations are difficult to sustain. Sexual abuse is predominantly committed by adult males on young girls (La Fontaine, 1990). Other than to talk more generally about the way abused girls become complicit in adulthood in covering up a spouse's abuse of a child, abused girls are less likely to become abusers in later life. A focus on individual abusers underlies the public fascination for the 'stranger danger' theme. I shall examine this later in my discussion of prevention strategies. But the idea that children are more likely to be abused by a stranger is a pertinent point here. Whilst all the evidence points to the child usually knowing the abuser, the abuser as stranger is a common myth which sharpens the idea that abusers are predatory loners with pathological failings. It is significant in drawing our attention away from thinking of abuse within familiar settings.

Although the evidence is limited, there is little doubt that the majority of abuse does take place within the home. This has often been used as a basis for a second category of pathology, the abusive family. The particular focus here is the way that types of families are characterized by weaker generational boundaries and inadequate forms of socialization. Finkelhor's (1988) research on sexual abuse in day-care centres in the United States is an attempt to overcome this focus on particular species or conditions of families. First, his evidence suggests that, although the family is a major site for the sexual abuse of children, it is not the only location.[1] Second, his theory of sexual abuse rests on what we might call 'structural opportunities'. Adults, by virtue of their status as carers or child workers, have the opportunity to take advantage of their positions of responsibility and authority, especially with very young children. Adults who 'care' for children are in a position to develop trusting relations with children on the basis of their personal, professional or biological commitments to working with children. The notion of trust does not simply inhere in the adult–child relationship but refers to an associated degree of autonomy and privacy in building up relations with children. The relations that adults have as professional carers with children are quite different from the trusting bonds formed between parent and child. However, adults in long-term professional set-ups where they come into regular contact with children quite often try and create a warm familial environment for those children they work with.

Regardless of this, from an abuser's perspective the issues are over relative closeness, degrees of autonomy and opportunities available. According to Finkelhor, these structural conditions make abuse possible and can be found to a greater or lesser degree in situations where adults have responsibilities for child care.

A third type of pathology revolves around the idea that social class or social geography are explanatory variables. The class dimension of child sexual abuse developed initially in the late nineteenth century in popular mythology on incest. It was believed that the 'lower orders' were more likely to practise incest because of their lack of culture and their relative closeness to primitive nature. The bourgeoisie, imbued with an evolutionary view of society, tended to see themselves on a higher developmental and cultural plain which insulated them from incestuous relations. Various modern versions exist which link class or social deprivation to either isolated or subculturally separate locations where incest and abuse are more likely to be found. Abusers are associated with an endless list of deprivations, among others, lack of education, propensity for crime, inappropriate lifestyles. Whilst popular mythology is hardly the basis for an analysis of child sexual abuse, the statistics, such as they are, seem to reflect this class dimension. The class basis of abuse has informed a variety of critical assessments of the child protection system (La Fontaine, 1990; Dingwall et al., 1995; Parton, 1996). Whilst there are a whole range of methodological problems in the measurement of abuse, the basic problem rests on relying on evidence that is biased towards working-class families. Parton's (1996) review of the most recent research commissioned by the Home Office, *Messages from Research*, highlights a bias in favour of lone parents and those on low incomes. Parton contends that these categories of people are the most vulnerable to state regulation and more likely to be counted in official statistics on child abuse. Dingwall et al. (1995) adopt a different mode of analysis but arrive at the same conclusions. The class–abuse connection becomes a consequence of political, administrative and practical decisions taken within the child protection system which 'select out' possible cases of middle-class abuse. La Fontaine (1990) goes a step further and attempts to demonstrate from her own empirical research that child sex abuse is not a working-class phenomenon. She compares her own study, a small sample of child sex abuse cases which were referred from the health and social services, with another study based on a representative sample of cases of adults claiming that they had been abused in childhood. La Fontaine points out the limitations of her comparison and discusses a range of methodological problems with her research. Despite these problems, her comparison reveals that there appears to be no correlation between class and child sexual abuse. She contends that children from all social classes are equally likely to become victims of sexual abuse.

Linking social class to child sexual abuse does not, strictly speaking, constitute a pathology of child sexual abuse. But the general principle of typifying and categorizing individuals or different sections of the population suggests that we are more likely to focus on sectors of the population, types of abusers and predisposing events. We are less likely to consider the classless nature of abuse, its location within a structure of opportunities for adults in positions of authority and trust to exploit. There is a tendency, then, among practitioners and academics to worry about the class backgrounds of particular families or the psychological inadequacies of particular parents rather than the position of adults or the general location of families in society. In effect, the framing of the problem of child sexual abuse in terms of protection and socialization does two things: it directs state intervention towards certain sectors of society, and it also serves to highlight the 'normality' of the nuclear family and the positions of the adult population in relation to children.

The Prevention of Child Sexual Abuse

Child Abuse Prevention Programmes (CAPP)

Whilst the overriding concern is to ensure that children are safe and under adequate protection, over the past few years there has been a mushrooming of initiatives dealing with the prevention of child sexual abuse. Some work is being done in Europe and we will look a little more closely at the 'Right to Security' programmes set up in Holland, but much of this new educational industry can be found in the United States. It is worth pointing out that there has not been universal acceptance of these programmes across the United States. In California, for instance, child abuse prevention programmes (CAPP) were repealed by the state government because it was felt that they would undermine young children's innocence (Hacking, 1991, p. 257). Yet a range of state- and school-based initiatives involving around two-thirds of all American children from pre-school age up to approximately the age of 12 have been introduced over the past few years (Rispens, Aleman and Goudena, 1997). Proponents of CAPP have tended to emphasize the advantages of school-based approaches, in that classrooms promote discussions between children as well as the more traditional didactic means of transmitting information. But educators draw on a variety of pedagogical approaches in trying to provide children with the knowledge, skills and resources which would help them deal with 'abusive advances' from adults. Some educators use theatre, either in the form of puppets or role play (Dhooper and Schneider, 1995). Others are using more discursive approaches in getting children to talk through the meaning of 'good' and 'bad' physical contact with adults.

Developed from two earlier American models – the 'Child Assault Prevention Project' and 'Feeling Yes, Feeling No' – the Dutch 'Right to Security' programme takes a more explicitly child-centred line and draws on other disciplines such as the health services. In their assessment of the programme, Taal and Edelaar (1997) state that in abusive situations children tend either to give in, or to avoid or confront the abuser. The programme targets children between the ages of 8 and 12 and through role play encourages them to adopt strategies for both defusing and avoiding threatening situations. The programme also invites pupils to discuss other potentially related non-sexual conflicts such as bullying. Although the focus of this programme is sexual abuse perpetrated by adults on children, children are being educated to deal with a whole range of threatening situations.

In Britain since the mid-1980s the organization Kidscape has been actively campaigning for a 'child's right to be safe'. Through literature that is geared towards both adults and children and through training and counselling services available to schools and communities, Kidscape has been working to improve the understandings that children of all ages have of their rights to physical integrity. Many of the themes found in the teaching material overlap with the American and Dutch programmes. There is an emphasis on children's being able to distinguish between 'good touches' and 'bad touches'. Children are to be encouraged to err on the side of saying 'No' if they are uneasy when 'trusted' adults approach them. There is the need to be cautious when approached by strangers, the 'stranger danger' theme. Importantly, the material stresses the distinction between 'good' and 'bad' secrets. The latter are carefully illustrated for both professionals and children through scenarios which place children in a series of dilemmas as to why a promise of confidentiality might have to be broken. In general, two approaches predominate: children are to be encouraged to discuss their feelings and anxieties with friends and trusted adults and there is an emphasis on the children protecting themselves.

Michelle Elliott, the founder and director of Kidscape, is well aware of the need to deal with existing assumptions about the position of children, in particular the way that we tend to differentiate between older and younger children. In her book *Preventing Child Sexual Assault: a practical guide to talking with children*, there is a separate chapter on how teenagers can deal with sexual assault, 'helping teenagers to protect themselves'. While the general thrust of the book is to encourage children to talk about threatening incidents and to help them to recognize legitimate touching and approaches from adults, teenagers are seen as having a degree of independence: they are more likely to spend time away from 'trusting adults' and to establish relationships with relative strangers. While there is little practical sense in advising young children to force their way out of abusive situations, teenagers are encouraged to learn self-defence and to use any physical and verbal force at their disposal to evade an attack. Adults are to recognize this independence whilst being aware that teenage children need to be believed in situations where there has been sexual assault.

CAPP and Childhood Competence

Preventive programmes are attempting to deal with the alleged increase in opportunities for child abuse. In the process these programmes are more likely to conceptualize abuse in terms of the child being subject to the will of the adult on the basis of the age difference. I argued in the previous section that the dominant paradigm of socialization tends to pathologize the problem of abuse. Kitzinger, on the other hand, contends that CAPP 'challenge us to re-assess our own use of authority as parents, strangers, friends and teachers' (1997, p. 169). We are getting close to a position in which the more general relationship between adult and child comes under the microscope. According to this view, the problem of child sexual abuse is more to do with the social structural position of children rather than any idea that particular children from particular families, communities and classes are more or less likely to become victims of abuse. In a recent critique of CAPP, Gary Melton (1996) contends that the programmes are doomed to failure because there is as yet no agreement on an aetiology of sexual abuse. The hidden nature of abuse and its problematic definition, according to Melton, make it difficult to identify any clear 'predisposing' factors. We are back to the idea of pathology here. In the absence of information which narrows down our population of prospective abusers, we are forced to target very broad groups of children. The need to identify specific causes of abuse clearly aids the categorization of children according to predisposing factors. Drawing on this kind of knowledge, CAPP might be directed towards specific groups of 'vulnerable' children. Michelle Elliott, on the other hand, sees the absence of any clear agenda for researching particular groups of children likely to be abused as grounds for ensuring that all children receive some sort of education on preventing abuse. In introducing one of her early books, *Preventing Child Sexual Assault*, she claims that 'the current universal definition and common characteristic of child molesters is that they molest children' (1985, p. 2). She goes on: 'molesters average 73 victims before they are caught and the risk of re-offending is extremely high (75 per cent)'. Elliott thus goes along with the broad thrust of the first part of this chapter: there are no solid research grounds for targeting specific groups of adults in society. We cannot therefore rule out the possibility that a starting point for the analysis of child sexual abuse is the social structural position of childhood. As I outlined in chapter 1, the social structural approach to childhood views children as members of a subordinate minority group within society with few rights and powers. Kidscape, like other CAPP, challenges the idea that certain types of children are more at risk than others. By asserting that all children need to be equipped to deal with the possibility of abuse, these initiatives also challenge the way that children's minority positions are sustained by ideas that endorse and naturalize adult–child relations in terms of authority and responsibility. Moreover, Elliott makes it clear that children might have to disobey 'trusted adults' if they feel that their physical integrity is being threatened. In an important sense, then, these initiatives, although directed at children, force adults, particularly parents to become more aware of their authority as a source of social power rather than a taken-for-granted aspect of their identities as parents.

Although Elliott is careful not to reject the role that adults play in preventing abuse, the idea of prevention moves away from the simple notion that, where children are more exposed to danger, adults should offer them protection by keeping them close and restricting their movements in public. Here we come into direct conflict with the idea of rescuing or reaffirming childhood discussed in chapter 1 and the notion of protection discussed earlier in this chapter. As Kitzinger (1997, p. 175) acutely observes:

> Just as early attempts to preserve endangered species relied on locking up specimens in zoos (rather than intervening against the 'man-made' attacks on their environment) so this child protection approach attempts to 'preserve childhood' by confining children behind bars.

I have referred to the way that a child's right to be safe, to have a degree of physical integrity, takes precedence over the traditional deferential role that the child plays. Taken-for-granted physical contact between parent and child is brought into question through programmes that emphasize 'good' and 'bad' touching. Hood-Williams (1990,

p. 166) refers to 'corporal' power: the routine access that parents have to a child's body which includes everything from hugging to physical punishment. Physical access, like social and political relations, is not reciprocal between subordinate and dominant groups. Notions of power imply at the individual level that children, like other members of minority groups, are acted upon and have fewer means of protecting themselves from the actions of other more dominant groups. Children are less likely to question the rights of access that adults have to their bodies, whereas adults might feel for instance, that they are being pestered by their children when they try to attract their attention by tugging their sleeves (Jackson in Epstein, 1993, pp. 320–321).

We can go further. The physical integrity of a minority group is, in theory, now protected by law. Although women, for example, may be more likely to suffer at the hands of violent partners and predatory male bosses, sexual harassment and spousal attacks are covered by the law of assault. Children, on the other hand, are still the one group in society not fully protected from the physical force of others. Although the definition of 'reasonable' force in relation to physical chastisement is becoming progressively narrower, parents still have the right to use violence when disciplining their children.[2] In general terms, CAPP's focus has been on the child's right to be safe. Yet much of the concern has been over how this right can be breached through sexual abuse. Now these programmes alert children to the way in which adults are able to turn a hug or a kiss into something more insidious. Children, in other words, are being sensitized to the ways in which inappropriate touching can be normalized. However, there is much less emphasis on how other activities such as punishment and discipline normalize other sorts of inappropriate touching such as physical chastisement. The 'violent' and sexual advances towards children are, strictly speaking, not comparable, in that physical punishment such as smacking, because of its legal status, can be used to normalize severe beatings, which are now much more clearly defined as physical abuse. As I discussed in chapter 2, if the 'rule of optimism' is still in operation, we tend to err on the side of believing parents when a hard smack might cross the grey area into physical abuse territory. Physical abuse of a sexual nature, on the other hand, is outlawed. The point I want to make here is that, despite these differences and despite the reticence of organizations like Kidscape to tackle corporal punishment, children are more likely to use the 'keeping safe' material to challenge all forms of inappropriate touching. Initiatives which encourage children to reflect on the kind of physical contact that their parents have with them will not always differentiate between sexual and 'physical' force. 'Bad touching' cannot simply be reduced to that which has a sexual intent or connotation. Furthermore, where these programmes are extended to include peer or sibling violence, children who learn to take more responsibility for their bodies, say in cases of bullying, are less likely to want to distinguish between the physical advances of adults and the violence handed out in the playground. Although the content of CAPP does not always make it clear how inclusive the intentions of the producers of the programmes are, there is the potential to use sex abuse programmes to sensitize children to all forms of adult physical power.

Children themselves are expected to become more assertive towards adults as a consequence of preventive education in the early years. It is worth pointing out that programmes such as Kidscape do not reject the importance of adults in supporting and protecting children – the teacher becomes an important reference point in many of the stories and scenarios found in the literature for children. Children are ultimately taught to rely on a core group of legitimate adults for support. Nevertheless, the onus is on children to 'establish their [own] network of trusted adults'. The emphasis is on encouraging children to 'trust their own feelings' and getting children to talk to adults suggests that children themselves are instrumental in setting up trusting relations with significant adult others (Elliott, 1989, p. 24). In this sense the idea of socialization involves a more active role for children in establishing such relations.

As well as challenging some of the taken-for-granted features of adult–child relations, these programmes also have the potential to undermine a range of common-sense and scientific assumptions which underpin the ambiguous ontological status of children (Jenks, 1982). I discussed in an earlier chapter the importance of the idea that childhood is the process whereby children move steadily towards the full social status of adulthood. There is no notion that children are fully 'developed' in ontological terms. That is, children are not commonly seen as social actors in their own right. In most senses children have a transitional being. This lack of status is reflected in the way in which children are subsumed within more powerful and more visible social institutions such as school and family. As I argued in chapter 1, children are invisible. A child's physical and psychological ontology are interpreted as a series of signs and symptoms that indicate possibilities of completion in the future. Within the socialization paradigm, the problem of sex abuse is commonly articulated in these terms, with signs and symptoms of abuse 'diagnosed' as possible indicators of future incompleteness. CAPP, on the other hand, are insistent that children deal with sex abuse as an immediate possibility; that dangers are ever-present and immediate in their consequences and that children have to be concerned for their current situations as siblings, peers and pupils. The material on prevention goes beyond the adult-centred world, where concern tends to focus on the long-term effects of abuse on the child's development towards full adult status (Kitzinger, 1997, p. 165). The programmes are necessarily 'short-term' in that they teach children to deal with the immediate possibilities of abuse in ways that are meaningful to them, rather than deal with the consequences the abuse might have later on in adulthood. In other words, these programmes work within a frame of reference which encourages children to be social actors in their own right, rather than social actors-in-being. As Barrie Thorne argues: 'children's interactions are not a preparation for life; they are life itself' (1993, p. 3). These programmes are not only child-centred but child present.

Childline

In Britain the charity Childline, set up in 1987, introduces a further dimension to the idea that children can be put in a position to challenge the imperative demands of adults. Through Childline children have access to a phone number which can be used in situations in which they feel threatened by others. In situations where children are being intimidated and abused by adults, or for that matter siblings and peers, the voice at the end of the phone becomes a third party, an outsider who gives children the opportunity to discuss their problems confidentially. Importantly, Childline operatives give out information and offer advice on how children might best deal with the problems they are facing. In situations where abuse has become or is likely to become a 'family secret', Childline can be the only practical source of support for children in dealing with the abuse.

The Limits of CAPP

Child abuse prevention programmes offer definite possibilities for children to take some responsibility for tackling the problem of sexual abuse and contesting the unchallenged position of adults. The programmes not only hint at a reappraisal of taken-for-granted notions of the way in which adults and children relate to each other, they also address the potential for professionals and social scientists to view children as ontologically established through membership of a minority social group. There are, though, problems for both children and adults with these programmes. There is first, the difficulty of overcoming the marked physical differences between young children and adults. Whilst the programmes do not pretend to provide solutions to the problem of abuse, an emphasis on the psychological responses that can be adopted by children and

the range of strategies for avoiding abuse tend to sometimes underesti-
mate and obscure the simple fact of biology that adults are in a much
stronger position to exert physical force. There is an interesting parallel
in recent debates within the new sociology of childhood. This is not the
place to go into too much detail, but it is worth noting that the shift
towards the reconstruction of childhood according to the child's social,
cultural and historical position has led some commentators to reappraise
the biological differences between adult and child.[3] With reference to
CAPP, encouraging children to 'say no' may not have quite the moral
and psychological force to counter the physical differences between adult
and child (La Fontaine, 1990, p. 223). It is easy to see how the problem
of abuse frames the child as vulnerable in both physical and emotional
senses for this is quite often the case in practice. Kitzinger (1997) discusses the kinds of resistance that child victims put up when being
abused. She argues that children are 'constantly acting to pre-empt,
evade or modify sexual violence' (1997, p. 173). In an important sense
she provides a useful corrective to the idea that the child is a passive
victim. Nevertheless, given the sheer physical force of the abuser, many
of the children in her study were only able to modify or blank out the
abuse; they were not able to avoid it.

One possible unintentional consequence of CAPP, one which follows
from the child's physical weakness, is the increase in guilt among children who are unsuccessful in applying their anti-abuse knowledge and
skills. Kitzinger (1997) cites the testimonies of adult survivors who
were convinced that saying 'no' or employing more elaborate attempts to
evade or limit the abuse made them believe that any subsequent abuse
was a result of their own failure to use their anti-abuse knowledge and
skills appropriately. In most cases the child's 'failure' was a result of the
physical presence and superiority of the abuser. Nevertheless, victims of
abuse have referred to the way in which the mismatch between their psychological preparedness and the offenders' social, psychological as well as
physical advantages, produces considerable anxiety among abused children and generates a kind of victim mentality whereby children blame
themselves for the abuse.

In many ways the emphasis on psychological preparedness, the possibilities for self-blame and the social context which presupposes the
child's lack of status make it very difficult to see how CAPP can counter
the individualism and pathologizing built into the problem of sexual
abuse that I discussed earlier in the chapter. The broader consequences of
CAPP might put pressure on schools and policy makers to recognize the
collective interests of children in being better informed and more
actively involved (see chapter 5). Yet the emphasis on psychological

preparedness could detract from an understanding of the structural features of child abuse. That is, children might learn to assert themselves in isolation with little or no knowledge of the common features of abuse: the structural notion of 'adult opportunity' and the special position that all children occupy within families.

Abuse as Process not Event

Taal and Edelaar (1997, p. 409) discuss the limitations of CAPP in the way that abuse is defined and theorized as an event or one-off advance and not the 'gradual trespassing [of] the child's boundaries'. Clearly it is much more difficult to alert children to the fact that abuse is an insidious process rooted in 'normal' family relations. I referred earlier to the potential of CAPP to help children to challenge inappropriate advances before they become normalized as 'special but secret routines' with a significant other. Yet several authors focus on the omission of issues such as incest for discussion from most of the programmes (Tutty, 1994; Melton, 1996). Many of the CAPP skirt around a common site for the abuse of children: the home. As was stated earlier, there are no definitive figures on the numbers of abusers, who their victims are and where the abuse takes place. There is a lack of consensus over the proportion of cases of abuse taking place within the home and there are no clear trends concerning whether children are more or less likely to be abused by a parent or stepparent. Whilst our common understandings of family still direct us to think that children are more vulnerable outside rather than inside the family, in summarizing the research on child sexual abuse, La Fontaine (1990) concludes by saying that 'children are most often abused in houses where they live, by the people with whom they live' (1990, p. 151). As I argued earlier (p. 64), adults with some recognized responsibilities for and authority over children have greater and easier access to children. Whilst this is one of the key factors which structures the abilities of adults to abuse, there are still far more opportunities for abuse to take place within the relatively private confines of the home.

We can return to the literature produced by Kidscape. The focus is on physical safety and the sensitizing of children to 'bad touching' from any adult (see p. 63). But there is a tendency to concentrate on the 'stranger danger' theme when contextualizing potential situations of abuse. Even where scenarios are set out which concentrate on the threat from a known 'adult', as in the reader for primary-school children *Willow Street Kids*, the known adult tends to be an uncle rather than a mother or father.[4] There is a lack of sustained information on the possible abusive advances from parents. It is difficult to know whether CAPP authors are tackling the issue obliquely so as not to alarm young children, whether they are forced to make their resource materials more palatable for schools and parents, or whether there is simply some sort of taboo on discussing incest. The implications of this are that CAPP should be more directly concerned with challenging the 'typical' situations of abuse within the home between parent and child. CAPP is thus promoted as a way of understanding abuse in social structural terms. That is, the social position of children within the home is more likely to open them up to a range of abusive situations which, because of the rights and authority of parents, gives them far fewer grounds for resisting.

In the earlier part of this chapter, I discussed how abuse undermines in all sorts of ways the common bonds of basic trust built up over time between parent and child. Basic trust is arguably best developed with a trusted and known adult who has an interest in ensuring that the child is safe, secure and loved. The difficulty with CAPP here is in finding a balance between making children aware of the way that abuse can arise out of 'normal' family relations and sustaining the idea that children need to place their trust in an experienced and loving adult, who tends to be a family member. One problem that Tutty (1994) had with her research was that where discussion of incest took place, there was some reticence to take in this information which could not simply be put down to children's lack of cognitive abilities. The children as well as those adults running the CAPP have problems in dealing with the possibility that 'trusted adults' could sexually abuse children. The issue can be resolved at a theoretical level by focusing on the idea of trust discussed earlier rather than on any *a priori* social relations that the child might have. In other words, the primary concern is to provide the building blocks for trust; the rights and sensibilities of parents to protect their children are secondary. We come back to the recent Children Act and the paramountcy principle. The child's welfare is the factor that determines issues of care and control. In theory, arrangements for looking after the child revolve around what is best for the child. If this means, in some cases, that parents have their customary rights suspended, then so be it. Yet at a practical and normative level the problem remains. The 'rule of optimism' still holds sway. The practical and existing social arrangements dictate that families are the dominant reference points. Judgements about whether children suspected of being abused are better off remaining within their families are probably still heavily influenced by the consequences of breaking the bonds that already exist between parent and child.

An alternative way of emphasizing the relational dimension to CAPP is to examine the position, influence and perceptions of the adult population. Randolph and Gold (1994) refer to 'secondary programmes', initiatives that specifically target the involvement of adult carers and teachers. They argue that these initiatives have limited appeal, particularly for parents, with parental take-up of these programmes much lower than for children. Rather ironically, children's minority status makes it much more likely that they will be exposed to programmes that are designed to empower them. The lack of choice open to children in school – their status as a 'captive audience' in class – means they have fewer ways of resisting CAPP.[5] Yet, independently of the logistics of presenting the material, professionals and educators are both loath to address abuse directly with groups of parents for fear of confrontation. Parents are less likely to want to discuss their potential status as child abusers with professionals. From the parental perspective there may also be a reticence to get involved with programmes because of an unwillingness to discuss the possibilities of abuse with their children. Randolph and Gold (1994) refer to the success some educators have in getting parents to discuss issues of abuse with their children. These same programmes have far less success in encouraging parents to discuss the possibility that abusers might be family members or friends. Again, we come across some sort of taboo within CAPP on openly and frankly drawing on the parent-as-abuser theme.

As I argued earlier (p. 71), trust is a key building block in the majority of non-abusing families. Researchers refer to the possibility that CAPP compromise this trust in that children become more sensitive to all forms of physical contact with adults (Taal and Edelaar, 1997; Rispens, Aleman and Goudena, 1997). Taal and Edelaar (1997) point to the success of the 'Right to Security' programme with older children, who felt more capable and confident in handling abusive advances. They also, interestingly, remark that this same group of older boys have problems with non-sexual touching at home. Another unintentional consequence of CAPP may be that children find it more difficult now to differentiate between good and bad touching and err on the side of a less 'physical' relationship with parents. The normal hustle and bustle of family life, the 'positive' and routine physical contact between various family members of families which comes within the broad rubric of trust is not so easily sustained.

In sum: we are faced with a range of problems associated with CAPP. But rather than reject the thrust of these programmes as some groups have done,[6] we might speculate that relations between children and 'trusted' adults are changing, with children having more say in family affairs. This could mean that the very fundamentals of family life, including the unconditional physical access that parents have to their children, are now more contested. CAPP might be seen as intrusive and potentially disruptive; it might also be seen as one regulated element within a broader opening up of families.

Identifying Child Sexual Abuse

Criminalization and Social Competence

In my discussion of professional accountability in chapter 2, I referred to criticisms of the recent Children Act. According to Parton (1996) the welfare of the child has been sacrificed by child workers for political and professional expediency. Resources and energy are disproportionately invested in protecting a small minority of high-priority cases of abuse. The problem lies with the processes of bureaucratization and criminalization. The child protection system has developed into a complex labyrinth of accounting procedures which ultimately protect the actions of child workers rather than tend to the 'needs' of children on the economic and social margins. A series of high-profile 'failures' within the system have sharpened the legal character of these procedures, reinforcing the demands on professionals to be seen to be making the right decisions whilst at the same time highlighting the legal and political dimensions of child protection. Moreover, the legal realm in particular, with its overriding interest in criminal justice, is said to have marginalized the considerations for the child's welfare. In the pursuit of justice and retribution children are now processed through an intimidating criminal justice system as 'evidential objects'. Our sensibilities towards children, particularly those in vulnerable positions, are sacrificed in the interests of a legal system driven by the imperatives of proceduralism.

With these concerns in mind, the Home Office, in conjunction with the Department of Health in Britain, published the *Memorandum of Good Practice* (1992). The specific aim of the document was to set out guidelines for the videoing of children's evidence introduced through the 1991 Criminal Justice Act. The broader aim was to try and balance the interests of justice with the child witness's welfare. This is clearly set out in the foreword. 'All too often the interests of justice have been frustrated – and the child further harmed by the legal process – because it has just not been possible for the child to cope with the full court appearance' (1992, p. i). Whilst there is a cogency and a professional urgency to this problem, in the following sections I want to address the political and legal implications that these trends have for the child's status as a competent social actor. There are legal and political demands placed on investigators of child sex abuse to produce more effective methods of identifying and convicting offenders. There are also equally compelling demands on legal professionals to promote the child's emotional and social well-being which, in effect, means trying to protect the child from the grim realities of the criminal justice system. The problem of child abuse has produced a conflict between justice and protection. But it has also produced some interesting, if possibly unintentional, consequences in terms of our understanding of children and the institution of childhood. This section then needs to be read alongside the prevention of child sexual abuse as a possible way of viewing childhood outside the conventional confines of adult protection.

Shifting Legal Rules and Practices

The very nature of child sex abuse, its commission within private surroundings, and the pressure that can be put on children to conceal the abuse from outsiders make it likely that a large proportion of abuse remains undetected (La Fontaine, 1990). Where children are in a position to claim that they have been abused, the 'private' nature of the offence usually means that the police, the social services and the courts have to rely on evidence from only one witness, the child victim. Furthermore, where the child is in a position to make a statement, the length of time between the initial allegation and court appearance places a huge strain on the victim. Spencer and Flin (1993) suggest that child witnesses have an average wait of 10.5 months between the defendant's arrest and the trial. This has implications for the numbers of cases that come to court. Cross et al. (1995), for instance, claim that, of cases forwarded to the prosecutor in four urban settings in the United States, only 54 per cent were carried forward to trial, significantly fewer than other categories of criminal offence.[7] Children's silence within the criminal justice system is also linked to a lack of guaranteed confidentiality that might be expected by adults in similar positions. Children become aware that inter-agency work means in practice that what they tell in confidence to a legitimate stranger will be discussed with others. Wattam (1997) comments that this is one of the reasons why children prefer the anonymity of organizations like Childline where they have more control over the kind of information they want to give and where confidentiality is guaranteed.

Yet what has particularly hampered the legal process here has been the way that child workers have tended to stress the 'doubtfulness' of the child's capacity to produce reliable accounts of situations and events. Until fairly recently most professionals working with children have had difficulties in accepting that children's accounts of incidents of abuse are truthful and accurate. If we address this issue within a judicial context, this scepticism has been codified through the corroboration ruling, which means that a child's evidence in court is inadmissible unless supported by evidence from another witness. Unlike the testimony of an adult, which can stand alone, a child's evidence on its own is deemed to be untrustworthy. Legally speaking, we can talk about the child as incompetent here.

Recent shifts in legal thinking suggest that it may not be quite so easy to differentiate between adults and children in terms of the latter's inability to act as a reliable witness. The 1988 Criminal Justice Act abolished the corroboration ruling for sworn and unsworn evidence from children. Cobley (1991, p. 369) points to the way in which judges still draw on the corroboration ruling in a more discretionary sense by tending to distrust a child's evidence on its own. Furthermore, in sex cases the corroboration rule still stands. The judge is legally bound to advise the jury that it is dangerous to convict solely on the evidence of witnesses who have been sexually assaulted. Yet, in principle, a child's evidence is now as valid as an adult's; the corroboration rule now applies to types of cases rather than the age of witnesses.

The presumption of the child's incompetence in court, another principle that limits the child's legal standing, has now been partially abolished. Until recently children under the age of 14 had to prove their competence before being allowed to give evidence. As with the corroboration ruling, the basic idea here was that young children could not be trusted to give truthful evidence under oath. Judges had to apply a competence test to child witnesses under 14 to find out whether they were sufficiently mentally fit to give evidence under oath; in effect, this meant testing children's ability to distinguish between telling the truth and telling lies. This often had the effect, in practice, of throwing out child abuse cases because the only witness to the abuse, the child, was unable to give sworn evidence. The 1991 Criminal Justice Act states that the child's competence no longer needs to be tested in criminal cases (a child's competence still needs to be assessed in civil proceedings).

New types of evidence from children are now admissible in court. The 1991 Criminal Justice Act allows video recordings of interviews between child victims and investigators conducted earlier in the proceedings to be brought into court and used as the prosecution's main evidence. Some courtroom practices have now changed in an attempt to accommodate the child as a reliable witness. The demeanour and dress of court officials have been adapted and less formal dress codes have been introduced. Screens in courtrooms have also been placed between the child witness and defendant so that the child feels able to give evidence without being distressed by the presence of the defendant. Whilst these innovations have been used with varying degrees of success, they do highlight the tension between the interests of criminal justice, in particular the procedural rights of the defendant to face his or her accuser in court, and the need to protect the child from the sometimes harsh consequences of the criminal justice system. Although this tension is being fruitfully debated in countries like Canada, the United States and Britain, other changes which relate to the presence of the child witness in court are further fuelling the debate. Children can now also give their evidence 'in court' through a video link-up where the child answers defence's questions in a separate room and the child's image and voice are transmitted to television screens in court. On the one hand, where children have to go through interrogation from a defence counsel, again the conventional legal rights of the accused to confront the witness in court are compromised by the video link-up. On the other hand, the admissibility of this kind of evidence counters the highly charged and contested nature of courtroom procedures and the possible traumatic effects this physical confrontation might have for the child.

The implications for the recognition of the child as a competent social actor are mixed here. In her report for the Scottish Office, Murray (1995) discusses the introduction of live television links (LTL) in criminal proceedings in Scotland from the child's perspective.[8] According to Murray, LTL was introduced to meet the needs of the child witness. These needs in practice were defined in protectionist rather than competence terms. She makes the point that children have little influence over decisions relating to the use of LTL. She cites the United Nations Convention on the Rights of the Child in that children are rarely consulted as to whether they consent to the use of LTL. Murray is also very critical of the competence requirement, in which the presumption is still that the child's character is unreliable. Despite the psychological evidence that accepts that children of any age are capable of performing reliably, and despite the abolition of the presumption of incompetence, there is a strong insistence that children have to prove their legal status.

Wattam (1992), on the other hand, refers to the fact that presumptions of incompetence need to be applied in specific legal contexts. Her ethnomethodology of child protection refers to a tension between structural properties such as age – the presumption of incompetence – and the routinization of case building. The routine and practical tasks of building a case in child protection involve a range of criteria including the age of the witness. Yet, taken together, the process of case building involves placing age in context. In effect, 'reliability' is a social construct dependent on a range of situational factors. Whilst there is a suggestion in her phenomenological approach here that legal rules in practice are always situationally applied, Wattam goes beyond specific situations and argues that, because the legal world now takes children seriously, legal personnel now feel more confident in applying the rules in favour of children. The key point here, however, is that professional and legal opinion seems to be shifting towards making fewer assumptions about the competence of the child as a witness. The issue, then, may not be whether children can accurately and honestly account for real-life situations; the significant questions now asked are how and where children's accounts are to take place. There is undoubtedly a difference here between the adult and child witnesses in terms of legal treatment. But where this might earlier have been a product of assumed ontological difference, it can now be seen as a pragmatic attempt at creating the conditions suitable for children to give evidence.

The Psycho-legal Realm

In an interesting recent article, White (1998) maintains that in spite of the increased role of the courts and the 'evidential' basis to child protection matters, psychology and the 'psy complex' are still influential in providing a knowledge basis for professional practice. White argues that Parton's thesis on the paradigm shift in thinking about child protection from the medical orientations of the 1960s to the criminalization of protection in the 1990s does not necessarily mean that the psy complex has lost its institutional power and intellectual appeal. Psychology is now more firmly linked to the individualistic and legalistic concerns of the courts and the social services. But the influence of psychology is not simply in its ability to provide evidence in socio-legal matters; it has arguably become instrumental in providing a knowledge base for the legal notion of the child as a reliable witness. For there now seems to be a growing professional, legal and academic consensus that 'the presumed gulf between the eyewitness abilities of children and adults has been seriously exaggerated' (Spencer and Flin, 1993, p. 287).

Before the psychological research that underpins the legal shift towards children's social competence is discussed, a word or two is required on the general position of children as research subjects. As I have argued on p. 57, strategies for child protection have conventionally drawn on a developmental or socialization frame which views children and adults as binary opposites. This assumption deprives children of any meaningful research status and normalizes countless invalid laboratory experiments. Children's lack of social status extends into the field of research. Their imputed incompetence influences the way that research can be carried out with children. In essence, the conventional position has been to see children as research objects who are worked 'on' rather than 'with'. O'Neill (1982) refers to the way in which research methodology already prejudges the child's competence and thus the researcher's results. The idea of experimentation can more easily take place if research subjects are assumed to be less complicated in the way they interact with the environment. The implied complexity of the adult mind, not to mention the ethical considerations of 'testing' adults, clearly makes it more difficult for experimental research on adults as far as the conduct of researchers and the precision of their results are concerned. Children, on the other hand, because of their inferior status and their asocial nature, and because of their simpler psychological make-up, are easier to work with and much more amenable to being measured. This imputed simplicity, in comparison with the complexity of an adult's mental makeup, implies that children's responsiveness to the environment is much more transparent and amenable to precise measurement. What this means is that laboratory testing of children seriously underestimates their cognitive abilities. The work of Dunn (1988) and Tizard and Hughes (1986) illustrates this point. Their research is based on more naturalistic settings – children were observed within the home playing and interacting with their parents and siblings. This kind of research provides a more authentic setting for assessing children's social skills, with children between the ages of 2 and 4 displaying the kinds of abilities normally attributed to children around the ages of 6 and 7 within a more conventional Piagetian frame. In developmental language, locating children within their natural habitat means that they are more likely to 'decentre' at a much earlier age than was suggested by Piaget. The authors contend that children are competent enough to understand the viewpoints of their parents and siblings, they take an avid interest in the way social rules are applied and the consequences for others of their application, and are able to make sense of how conflicts between their parents and siblings are played out and resolved.

Drawing more on research that focuses on children's cognitive abilities, Spencer and Flyn (1993) seem to come to the same sorts of conclusions about young children's levels of competence. They argue that cognitive and developmental research has moved away from the idea that the child is cognitively and morally inferior to adults. In their review of recent psychological evidence, they propose that a range of cognitive factors have traditionally separated children from adults which scientifically substantiated the moral superiority of the latter over the former. If we turn to the conventional binary division between adult and child, Spencer and Flin (1993) produce a long and detailed review of psychological assumptions which underpin this division in terms of relevant research and possible implications for the legal system. I summarize these assumptions in the following.

Children are unreliable: The emphasis here is on the child's ability to retain information and recall in sufficient detail and degree of accuracy events that may have taken place months earlier. According to the research, children cannot normally retain as much information as adults and are therefore less likely to recount events that took place in the past with any accuracy. Research on 'free recall' – the ability to remember everything connected to an event without prompting – shows that children are possibly inferior in relation to the quantity of information that they can give on any past event. Yet, in terms of quality or accuracy of recall, there are no significant differences between adults and children. The authors counter the assumption of children's incompetence by referring to a range of factors which determine the reliability of memory, one of which may be age difference. If we take into account the way that the information is elicited, that is, the interview situation, the quality of data offered by the child is not drastically inferior to the information given by adults in similar situations. The authors correctly point out that, when adult witnesses are subjected to the kinds of pressures placed on child witnesses, it can lead them to distort events. Finally, we referred earlier to the slowness of the legal process, which has an impact on the quantity and quality of evidence given. The problem of reliability can partly be alleviated if the legal process were slightly more compressed.

Children are more suggestible: The idea that children are more easily led than adults is a familiar notion. Based on the idea that children are less experienced, some would say less cynical, children are more likely to go along with the suggestions of more influential others. In legal terms, this is said to make children poor witnesses in that their truth claims can always be distorted by more mature and experienced adults with particular vested interests. Again, the evidence is inconclusive. In very general terms the research demonstrates that young children can be duped into erroneously describing incidents and people that they thought they had met. On the other hand, where the research specifically examines children's abilities to remember people and events linked to abusive situations, they are much more likely to stick with their version of events despite the pressure that the interview situation puts them under. Yet again, the key theme here is the need to balance three factors: the subordinate position of children – their desire to please and obey adults; the need to end a distressing process of recapitulating events which make it more likely that children will distort the truth; and the need to create less intimidating interview conditions. Again, the research indicates that the adult–child dichotomy is much less rigid than was first thought: both adults and children can be swayed, according to circumstances.

The fact–fantasy debate: This has been one of the more controversial issues, with claims and counter-claims made against adult abusers on the basis of whether child victims imagine rather than experience abuse. Spencer and Flin (1993, pp. 309–312) locate this debate historically in the witchcraft trials of the sixteenth and seventeenth centuries in Britain and the United States, where children became chief witnesses in a series of trials of alleged witches. The authors argue that, although historians now claim that the role of children has been exaggerated in condemning women to the stake on the basis of their accounts, there is a historically recurring idea that children's imaginations get the better of them in that they fantasize about things that happen to them. The recent events in Orkney and Rochdale attest to the persistence of this question. In both cases parents were accused of ritual abuse on the basis of accounts given by their children. Children alleged that they were present at and sometimes forced to take part in a series of bestial and sacrificial sexual acts with groups of adults. With respect to reported cases of ritual abuse, there is no consensus among academics or professionals as to the veracity of claims made by both children and adults referring to their childhoods.[9] Yet these rather sensationalist events, taken with the alleged rise in children watching so-called 'video nasties', tend to perpetuate the idea of the suggestible child easily prone to exaggeration and fantasy. Spencer and Flin (1993, pp. 317–318) argue that fantasy and play are key elements in the very young child's daily repertoire of activities but that incidents of sexual abuse are of a different order of event, provoking quite distinct and disturbing accounts from children. In other words, although young children might be prone to making fantastic imaginative leaps, any attempt that a child makes to describe an abusive situation can only mean that children are trying to reveal something that is completely out of the normal, something that they are incapable of making up.

Children lie whilst adults tell the truth: The contention that children are more likely to lie than adults is based on the notion that children's lies are more easily detected than any notion that children are inherently less truthful, according to Spencer and Flin (1993). Indeed, we are more likely to spot children telling 'whoppers' than discern the sophisticated but untruthful claims made by adults. Furthermore, the rate at which children withdraw allegations of abuse is often linked to the notion that they are more likely to fabricate accounts of events. Cobley (1991) argues that this can be put down to the kinds of pressures children are under from family members to withdraw and a not implausible assumption held by the child witness that he or she is less likely to be believed by the authorities. There is little evidence to suggest that children are more likely to make false allegations than adults. There is also a sense in which what is being assessed here is not so much the veracity of children as against that of adults, but the nature of the claims made. Spencer and Flin quote various eminent cases from the past where women and children are grouped together because they are more likely to complain about incidents of a sexual nature. Witness reliability, then, is linked to sexual abuse, rape and sexual harassment, crimes which are notoriously difficult to prove because of their sensitive nature and lack of witnesses.

Children are morally incompetent: This notion rests on the idea that children are less likely to comprehend the gravity of the distinction between truthfulness and dishonesty and therefore less likely to take their testimony seriously. The authors refer to the way that judges often test the moral competence of children by asking them about how they know things to be truthful (see p. 75). Reliability here rests more on their ability to articulate a definition of truthfulness than any notion that they might be likely to lie in court. In other words, although children may have a limited knowledge of morality, it does not follow that they are more likely to behave 'immorally' in court. The position of adults is germane here in that adults are not subject to any competence test. It is assumed that they can articulate the difference between truth and falsehood. Discovering that adults have a perfect understanding of morality does not make it less likely that they would lie in court.

Egocentricity: This final factor directly relates to the developmental notion that children learn to become less egocentred as they grow up. Spencer and Flin strangely spend much less time on this factor but conclude that egocentrism and, by implication, an ability to decentre is context- rather simply age-specific. They also add that self-absorption leads to a reduced awareness of what others are doing and the social and moral significance of others' actions and that there is ultimately an inability always to differentiate between key and peripheral events. The authors argue that, whilst very young children may find it difficult to decentre and therefore have difficulties in detaching themselves from things happening around them, this is a state of affairs that affects some adults. Importantly, for certain groups in society egocentrism is a key characteristic of adulthood.

The authors state that in their relations with children, adults often display an inability or unwillingness to see the child's point of view. Adults' self-absorption manifests itself in the way that they do things to and for children without any attempt to gain the assent or the opinion of children. With respect to children, adults are very egocentric.

The research taken as a whole is by no means conclusive, but an absolute distinction between adult and child in cognitive terms is no longer sustainable. There now is tendency to think in terms of a continuum of degrees of competence that both adults and children can be measured against. Thus children and adults are more or less truthful, reliable and suggestible. It all depends on how witnesses are handled, by whom and at what distance from the abuse in both temporal and spatial terms.

Children as Responsible Legal Subjects

Up to now I have been discussing the child as a witness within the legal system. A key policy theme has been the need for politicians, practitioners and academics to devise strategies for protecting children and limit their degree of vulnerability. Equally urgent demands are now being made to deal with problems relating to children who sit, as it were, on the opposite side of the legal fence, the problem of children as offenders. As I mentioned in chapter 2, one of the problems with the children's rights lobby is the rather one-sided view taken on rights. Children are to be empowered through the development of procedures that ensure that their opinions count. The children's rights lobby takes a proactive line. Children are to be put in positions to take action against those who fail to accept their right to be heard. An underlying assumption here is that children should be given rights because there are no sound logical or scientific reasons for denying them rights if these are based on the criterion of incompetence. It follows that, if children are to be granted more rights of a self-determinist variety, then we have to assume that they accept the consequences of their new-found status. There seems to be little within the discourse on children's rights that follows the logic of childhood competence in suggesting that children are responsible legal agents.

With reference to the notion of the child as a *responsible* legal witness, Spencer and Flin (1993, pp. 70–73) address the issue of compellability. They examine the extent to which the *quid pro quo* for recognizing children's competence is the requirement that they cannot refuse to be witnesses. Competence in the judicial sense presupposes responsibility and this applies more or less to child witnesses. Those witnesses who refuse to answer questions in court are in contempt of court. This is a criminal offence and therefore punishable. The 1998 Crime and Disorder Act strengthens this position. The jury are now allowed to draw inferences from the child witnesses' silence in court, whether this silence applies to children who refuse to answer questions in court or children who refuse to appear as witnesses. These rules do not apply to children under the age of 10, who are not considered to be criminally responsible. In legal terms they cannot be punished.

The corollary in legal terms of the child as a reliable witness is the child as offender. If we refer to the Bulger case, there were extreme public reactions to the two 10-year-old boys convicted of murdering Jamie Bulger. Calls for intemperate forms of retribution – hanging was one suggestion – were countered by more measured concerns for the institution of childhood. In the former case action was demanded because the crime was so horrific – the mutilation of an infant – but the demands for much stronger sentences than might be given to adults committing the same sort of crime reflect the ideas that the two child offenders were deviant species of childhood (Jenks, 1996). Here the calls for leniency and understanding were attempts to retrieve the situation by suggesting that the two offenders were only children and could not be treated in the same way as adults who had committed serious offences. In the event the Home Secretary, subject to public and political pressure, took the unusual step of intervening and lengthening their sentences from 10 to 15 years. In one sense, the Jamie Bulger issue brings us back to the notion that childhood is in crisis. According to Postman (1982), child crime is an important indicator of the disappearance of childhood: in the United States there has been a rise in the proportion of crime committed by children and the nature of the crimes has changed. Children as a category of criminals commit more crimes than before and more of these crimes are of a 'grown-up' nature. Whilst we need to query Postman's statistical analysis – and there is no significant factual basis to the idea that the Bulger case is illustrative of the same trends in Britain – what he may be alluding to is a set of perceptions which evoke a more generalized notion of Murray's underclass 'man-child'. The Bulger case, in other words, is symbolic of a much stronger public fear of crime and the idea that children are now more vulnerable as both offenders and victims. In another sense, the case is an interesting illustration of our confused thinking on how to deal with young children who commit serious crime.

In other legal situations there is a clearer sense that children might be expected to take responsibility. We can illustrate this point with reference to the 1993 Sexual Offences Act. The presumption that boys under the age of 14 are incapable of sexual intercourse has now been abolished.

In effect, this means that the child as offender is more fully recognized in cases of alleged rape. A recent illustration of this was a 13-year-old boy from the north of England who was convicted of raping a 5-year-old girl and placed on the National Register of Sex Offenders for life (*The Times*, 30 May 1998). There is no notion that the law was merely reflecting changes in the age of male sexual capacity. Clearly, boys much younger than 14 have always been capable physiologically of sexual intercourse. What we have here is a legal recognition that boys under the age of 14 are capable of comprehending what the act means. The case in England revolved around whether the boy intended to rape the girl. Competence here is attributed to children on the basis of their cognitive and moral abilities. It reflects the idea that they are old enough to take responsibility for their actions.

Butler-Sloss and After

Spencer and Flin (1993) maintain in their exhaustive review of the research on child witnesses, that there are now unambiguous psychological grounds for listening to children. Whilst some of this research on children's competence connects with changes to the legal rules on children, they contend that the whole lengthy process of child abuse proceedings needs to be overhauled. Careful consideration needs to be given to the various points along the time-frame between initial complaint and court appearance (we might also want to include the post-trial period) when children's accounts and opinions are solicited. This point seems to underpin the Butler-Sloss Report commissioned in the aftermath of the Cleveland events. Several recommendations were made to improving relations between child witnesses and the various professionals involved in abuse cases. The report refers to problems that children have with 'disclosure' interviews, where professionals assume that the child has something to reveal and a range of verbal strategies are deployed to extract this information. Criminal justice imperatives here are to be counterbalanced by more 'facilitative' approaches where there is more importance attached to making the child feel comfortable, where interviewers are to work at the child's pace and where the setting of the interview is to be less threatening. The inter-agency dimension is another focus of the report, largely because of how the conflicts between health and social services and the police surfaced during Cleveland. A much broader perspective is advocated here, with a more inclusive approach to working with children. Teachers, for example, are incorporated within the network of child support. Recommendations are made for clearer lines of communication and support between agencies. There is also to be more training to raise awareness of preventive issues, with more systematic training for professionals involved in interviewing children.

The criminal justice approach, in its emphasis on procedure and search for convictions, is said to undermine the imperatives of welfare in that the processing of children through the system exposes them to unnecessary harm. It reinforces their already vulnerable state as victims of abuse. I am suggesting here that the opposition is slightly overstated. If we address welfare in terms of competence as well as protection, then in an important sense the criminal justice system converges with children's interests. To process children through the legal system as 'evidential objects' is to make assumptions about their capacities as social actors. I am also suggesting that the conception of the vulnerable child obscures somewhat the distinction between the type of case and types of client. Undoubtedly children are vulnerable, and may be doubly so if, to paraphrase Butler-Sloss, they are seen merely as objects of concern rather than human subjects by criminal justice agencies. At the same time child sex abuse is part of a broader category of sex crimes which heighten the vulnerable status of all victims because of the assumptions made about the nature of the crime and subsequent legal treatment. Irrespective of whether we are talking about children or adults, the problems of victims of sex crimes are similar: the lack of third parties to the incidents; the emotionally charged nature of the crimes and the secretive nature of sex in society.

Conclusion

It might be useful to summarize the key themes of the chapter under the three main headings.

Protection. The concept of socialization viewed from within the rubric of child protection constrains our viewpoint on the problem of child sexual abuse. It does this by generating a pathology of abuse by focusing our attention on individual families. It also normalizes the power and authority of adults and sanctifies the role of the family. In these terms the problem of child sexual abuse generates a conception of the *vulnerable passive child.*

Prevention. The drive towards the prevention of abuse has given children and child workers the opportunity to undermine the implicit paternalism within the child protection system. Despite the fact that child abuse prevention programmes are initiated within a context of child protection, we are presented here with a much more contested view of childhood. Vulnerability here is confronted by the *competent and challenging child.*

Identification. The political and legal imperative to identify child sexual abusers has generated a tension between the need to push the child through the legal system and the need to protect him or her from the traumatic effects of the child abuse case. Whilst the latter has compromised the model of the child as a fully formed legal subject, the former has generated the idea of the child as a *reliable social actor.*

It is difficult to know whether the problem of child sexual abuse has generated real possibilities for viewing children as a common social group separate from their families of origin. It is also unclear how far we can take the notion of the socially competent child. The overarching imperative is to protect. This is partly due to the influence of 'family', 'authority' and 'responsibility' as organizing principles for viewing children as vulnerable and dependent social actors-in-waiting. It is also partly as a result of professional demands to define clearly the lines of responsibility and accountability discussed in the previous chapter, with general points of contact directed downwards towards 'children at risk'. A third factor relies on the largely untested and unquantifiable notion of public opinion. Given the added impetus to blame and pathologize, adults' relations with children probably err on the side of extreme caution.

Yet in the analyses of prevention and identification, childhood seems to be much more contested. I am suggesting that the pressure policy makers, public commentators and professionals are under to protect the child have produced alternative, possibly unintentional models of childhood that converge on ideas developed within the new sociology of childhood. Notions of child competence and responsibility are developed within the criminal justice system for pragmatic and political reasons. Child abuse prevention programmes, driven by the same pragmatic impulses, assume degrees of childhood competence whilst challenging the notion of the innocent child. Whilst the paradigm of socialization is not being directly challenged, by implication children are being encouraged to be more active in preventing and identifying child abuse.

4 Childhood, Agency and Education Reform

Introduction

In this and the following chapter I want to examine the way in which childhood is currently viewed from an educational perspective. In chapter 2 I argued that child-care and education policy have been radically overhauled, with a much sharper focus on what parents do to and for their children in terms of rights and obligations. Policy stops short of being an unambiguous parents' charter. Although concepts such as parental responsibility and professional accountability position child workers more defensively *vis-à-vis* the individual interests of the parent as consumer, parents are now more subject to external scrutiny of their child-rearing obligations. Moreover, if we focus on child care, social policy complicates lines of adult responsibility by entertaining the possibility that children are competent social actors. Another important factor, then, which restricts any notion that parents are all-powerful when exercising their responsibility is the idea that the child's wishes need to be taken into consideration in matters relating to his or her home life. I want to return to education policy in this chapter and discuss what 'the wishes and feelings of children' amount to from an educational perspective. The conventional view is that schools play a formative role in their lives. In trying to locate the position of children within the broader social structure, which the notion of agency presumes, I assess the extent to which children themselves are formative within a changing school environment. Given that certain aspects of education reform suggest a shift towards individual agency, namely. the attention paid to the rational consumer of education, questions on the position of pupils within the education system are particularly pertinent.

Childhood and Agency

In chapter 1 I outlined a key feature of the new sociology of childhood, the situating of children's lives in terms of the concept of social agency. Certain abilities and competencies are attributed to children so that they are now recognized as influential participants within a variety of social contexts. I drew on James, Jenks and Prout's (1998) conceptual framework in identifying two ways in which children and agency are brought together. First, there is the notion of the 'tribal child', whereby children are active and formative within their own social world of the peer group. Second, the notion of the 'social structural' or 'minority group' child denotes that children's behaviour and ways of thinking need to be located within the broader social structure. Children's action here is constrained by virtue of their membership of a marginal social grouping. As I argued in chapter 1, a key aim of the new sociology of childhood is to bring this marginal status to the foreground and identify possible and actual means through which children are seen as 'agentic'.

This brings us to the position of children within the system of education and schooling. If we focus on the tribal child, the school would seem to be the arena *par excellence* for the examination of children as social agents. First of all, children are a highly segregated and regulated social grouping and therefore more amenable and accessible to the research community (James, Jenks and Prout, 1998). They are more easily identifiable as a social grouping in school. Second, this segregation allows them to mix with other children of their own age and ability. There is thus a degree of homology between children within their peer groups which enables us to observe the way they bully, negotiate, manipulate, draw on a whole range of social strategies as if they were constructing their own micro-society. School ethnographies demonstrate children's abilities beyond their 'developmental' capabilities (Epstein, 1993), and in an epistemological sense these abilities are located within what we term 'social meaning systems'. Children's activities are driven by interpretive schema in much the same way as adults make sense of the social world.

Whilst the 'tribalizing' of childhood centres the analysis on what children do and how children 'develop' in their own terms, in this chapter I am interested in children's broader relations within the predominantly adult world: I shall pursue children's schooling from a social structural perspective. Here what is of primary importance is the fact of segregation and regulation in school. This approach tends to focus on questions about how children deal with the structures imposed on them by adults. Within schools children are less creative, less able to construct meaning, because their school lives are more or less determined by curricular and behavioural rules and structures. This control in school is indicative of the broader social field for children. The school reflects, if not amplifies, the child's lack of social status. Children pass through school as they pass through the various developmental stages *en route* to something grander and more established.

An emphasis on structure brings out the way in which society constrains social action. The education system and the school need to be seen as limiting the possibilities for viewing children as social agents. First of all, the school accentuates the subordinate status of children in the way that rules, values and working routines are oriented around the need to act on and position children. James, Jenks and Prout refer to the temporality of childhood. They state that:

> schooling imposes complex temporal schedules which, through their intersection, structure daily, weekly and yearly cycles and create, for children, different spatial and temporal constraints and possibilities in relation to their school work which must be negotiated with parents and teachers
>
> (1998, p. 75)

This temporal structuring can be broken down into two forms: global and routine time. A 'global' notion of time refers to the age-grading system built in to most education systems within advanced societies which determines the relations children have with their peers and teachers. We return to the influence of developmental psychology. The linking of biological development to educational growth means that children's peers are determined on the basis of chronological age. Friendship patterns and access to significant adult figures in school are determined by age. Furthermore, Piaget's idea of a 'genetic epistemology' sets out a clear relationship between physiological growth and how this structures the nature of learning, the acquisition of knowledge and the overall development of the cognitive and moral self. The 'staging' of education also structures the ways in which children are acted upon by adults. The preparation of adults for teaching, the practices of ancillary educational services and the routines of local-, school- and classroom-level administrations are suffused with ideas that position children on the basis of age.

Routine time is a less abstract notion of temporal structuring, manifesting itself in the more immediate and constraining force of the school timetable. Children's day-to-day activities – their use of time and space – are determined by the timetable. Timetables reflect the educational, political and moral priorities within local and national contexts. There is, globally speaking, some variation between the form and content of timetables. Nevertheless, from the pupils' vantage points there is still the same sense of temporal structuring in that, within the timetable, pupils are supposed to know where they are, what they are doing and when they are allowed to act. The timetable acts as a kind of social and cultural map in that rules and regulations regarding what children are able to do – the quality and quantity of social contacts and their abilities to assert themselves in relation to school work and school leisure – ultimately conform to the temporal demands of the school day.

Second, despite children on occasion having a marginal influence on the delivery and content of what they are offered in class, what they learn and how they learn are given to them through the school curriculum. Whether the curriculum is structured by moral, economic or social imperatives, children's moral and intellectual commitments and skills are determined by the content of classroom teaching and the regulative strategies adopted by teachers in conveying the curriculum. This is reinforced by the different forms which measure and monitor these commitments. Finally, the timetable and the curriculum are overlaid with codes of conduct and modes of self-display, with rules and regulations which are sometimes formalized, sometimes overtly obvious to pupils. Behaviour, dress and speech codes limit what pupils can do in class. Arguably, these codes extend now into the relatively autonomous space of the playground. Again, there is some degree of variation in the forms that they take. Yet the net effect is to limit the possibilities which demonstrate children's social competence.

A comment on pedagogies that aim to liberate children is needed here. With specific reference to 'child-centredness', there are grounds for viewing a child-centred pedagogy as offering children more opportunities to innovate than, say, a more teacher-centred approach which physically dominates the child's use of time and space. On the other hand, the emphasis on the 'individual child' and his or her needs and the propensity for 'self-discovery', particularly when underpinned by a developmental frame, might have the opposite effect. Walkerdine (1984) brings this out in her critique of developmental psychology within primary schooling.

> It is perhaps the supreme irony that the concern for individual freedom and the hope of a naturalised rationality that could save mankind should have provided the condition for the production of a set of apparatuses which would aid in the production of the normalised child. It is the empirical apparatuses of stages of development which of all Piaget's work has been most utilised in

education. It is precisely this, and its insertion into a framework of biologised capacities, which ensures that the child is produced as an object of the scientific and pedagogical gaze by means of the very mechanisms which were intended to produce liberation.

(1984, p. 190)

Walkerdine refers to the way children are positioned through a process of 'normalisation'. Children are defined in terms of their relationship to a series of precise educational and developmental markers, educational norms. They assume the importance of cultural norms so that children on the boundaries of these markers, those, for example, designated 'special needs', are seen to have more general problems with their relationships and understandings of the social world.

Whilst I would not wish to give the impression that pupils are the only section of the school population determined by the timetable, the curriculum and the general structure of schooling, there is clearly a sense in which adults involved within the educational world (as I will outline in the following sections, this is a much more inclusive grouping of adults) have a much greater degree of autonomy. Teachers as well as pupils have increasingly more of their time and space absorbed within the new structures derived from recent reforms. However, as I discussed in chapter 1, Oldman's (1994) notion of 'child work' rests on the continuing exploitation of children in the interests of creating more economic opportunities for workers and professionals within the field of education. We can also refer again to the developmental frame and the way in which it denies children a clearly defined social ontology. Teachers, on the other hand, establish themselves professionally and culturally as a clearly identifiable social grouping. The school is their domain or, as Cullingford (1991, p. 171) tersely puts it, 'schools remain the worlds of teachers in which children are temporary guests'.

It would probably be more productive to integrate both 'macro' and 'micro' approaches.[1] Connections need to be made between the meaning systems found within the playground and the structure of the education system. To some extent I shall try to link the playground role of pupils with the adult-centred and rule-bound routines within schools in the section on peer mediation in chapter 5. More generally, within the sociology of education, ethnographic work has focused on the way that young people, because they are competent enough to organize themselves, can threaten the authority of adults in school. Since Willis' seminal work in 1977 a major thrust of the sociology of deviance in schools has been to identify the threat to adult interests by deviant schoolchildren. Yet, if we accept Davies' (1994) distinction between

subversive and transformative action, the deviance observed and catego-
rized by sociologists tends to be of the former variety. Much of the
sociology of deviance has not been overly concerned with the transformative potential of classroom deviance, at least not in terms of the status
of children.[2] We are a long way from being able to identify how these
kinds of activities are shifting educational agendas towards children's
interests.

In this chapter I address the pupils' position within the school as an
instance of the broader state of play for children as a social grouping.
Although there is no attempt to deny the creative potential identified in
small-scale settings, I will concern myself with an outline of the macro
picture for children as pupils in relation to general shifts within education systems. The analysis of schooling and education reform
concentrates mainly on the British schooling system, but from time to
time I draw on similar trends found in other countries. I shall examine
four key elements of reform: the provision of schooling, school organization, curricular and pedagogic matters and relations between schools
and the broader community.

School Provision

Notwithstanding the centralization of the curriculum, the influence of
consumer choice and school selection discussed in chapter 2 suggests a
degree of local influence over the provision of education in England and
Wales. Parents are in a stronger position to choose their children's
schooling. They also have more influence over whether their children's
schools become more independent from local authority control through
'opting out' and, finally, we can point to the way that head teachers have
been given more latitude in managing their schools. What is of interest
here is that, despite the emphasis on more localized agencies, we come
up against the age-old limits of individualism in that the recipients of
schooling, the pupils, because of their subordinate positions within
families, are not considered to 'consume' education (Harris, 1994). If we
consider the possibilities for schools to 'opt out', it is parents rather than
pupils who are canvassed for their support. A school's decision to apply
for grant-maintained status, which, in theory, is supposed to give
schools more autonomy from local education authorities, ultimately
rests on the outcome of a vote by parents from within the school
constituency. The notion of an informed choice or vote is based on
information which addresses parents as the responsible parties.
Information from schools is addressed to parents; key events relating to
school choice – and for that matter school policy – involve parents, not

pupils, and the league tables which are supposed to produce equivalent comparative data on schools' performances are published through the adult media, the newspapers.

Predictably, most research on school choice follows the same adult-centred pattern, with little consideration given to the child's involvement in school choice. Where children are seen to be involved, the child's 'voice' is analysed indirectly through what parents say about their children's involvement (see, for example, Thomas and Dennison, 1991). That said, there have been some notable exceptions. Meighan (1977) wrote very generally from this vantage point about 'the pupil as client' in the 1970s. Findings from research that have centred on the pupils' perspectives interestingly suggest less adult-centred patterns. Where the research has focused on outcomes, the majority of decisions are based on the joint endeavours of parents and children (West, Varlaam and Scott, 1991). Research has also taken a less rationalistic line and focused on the process of choice (Gorard, 1996; Carroll and Walford, 1997). Choice here is linked to a more complex network of interactions over time involving children, parents, teachers and members of the local community. It is worth noting here that within this process of choice children are influential agents. If we go beyond policy and in many cases research convention, we can identify children making significant contributions to the process of school choice. But the legal context and the whole tenor of information from schools and through the media clearly locates adults as the influential agents.

School Organization

The same pattern emerges in the way schools are run. Education reform in Britain has eliminated any formal rights to pupil participation at the school level. Jeffs (1995) and Osler (1994) argue that the 1986 Education Act contravenes the principles of the United Nations Convention on the Rights of the Child. The Act, whilst increasing the representation of parents on school governing bodies, removed the influence that pupils had in drafting school regulations by dismissing them from these bodies. There is almost an inverse relationship here between the changing fortunes of parental and pupil influence. As parents appear to have become progressively more influential both as consumers of education and governors of schools, pupils have lost the few bargaining powers they once had.

In educational terms, there would appear to be no official rationale for this loss of student influence. An illustration from the British context provides us with some grounds for thinking that student influence, rather than being an outcome of more localized control, is actually morally and politically counter-intuitive. The 1986 and 1988 Education Acts devolved certain responsibilities from central government to individual schools through what is called the Local Management of Schools (LMS). Among other things, this means that instead of local government determining budgets for individual schools, the schools through their governing bodies manage their own finances. In 1997 these forces were brought into play when schools were required to manage an overall reduction in funding from central government. For many schools this involved a cost-cutting exercise in which governing bodies were in the position of having to reassess the contracts of some teachers. Thus lay members of the community became embroiled in deliberations over the merits of individual teachers. This may be a good example of the way education reform has given local communities a degree of control over the education process. It is also clearly an example of how pupils, because of their status as incompetent social actors, are seen to be inappropriately positioned on school governing bodies.

If we turn, more broadly, to pupil participation and consultation, again the same trend is apparent. The Children's Rights Development Unit (CRDU) (1994), in a recent critique of Britain's engagement with the United Nation's Convention on the Rights of the Child, states that recent education reform provides no framework for pupil involvement in school structures. This is set against two other recent national policy statements which promote greater child involvement: the 1989 Children Act and the Elton Report, the most important review of discipline in schools in recent years. The former is discussed in chapter 2. The latter is of more interest here, for it focuses directly on what is normally seen as a quintessentially adult preoccupation, the business of keeping order in schools. As I set out in chapter 1, a key feature of modern childhood is the positioning of children in relation to adults in terms of the former's need for moral guidance and boundary setting from the latter. Translated into teacher talk as 'classroom management', this notion seems to be a key feature of the way in which the teachers define their professional sense of self in the classroom. The 'good' teacher is someone who impresses him or herself on the class in a variety of overt and covert ways.

The Elton Report is interesting because it recommends that children's views need to be taken into account when schools develop policies on discipline. The report is quite explicit in recommending greater pupil involvement: schools need to encourage 'the active participation of pupils in shaping and reviewing the school's behaviour policy' (1989, p. 144). The CRDU points to a distinct lack of structure within which pupils have any say over the kinds of sanctions imposed on them in school.[3] Now it would be fair to say that some schools have followed this recommendation in involving their pupils in the setting of codes of conduct in school. To illustrate: Fogelman (1991) states that a majority of what were then ILEA (London) secondary schools have set up school councils, with pupils participating. But there is nothing contained in national policy that gives pupils a degree of control over the form and content of schooling. I will address the role of school councils when I discuss the Labour government's recently published advisory document on the teaching of citizenship in chapter 5. As yet, and for the purposes of the discussion here, there are no formal means of redress for students. Moreover, the introduction of mechanisms for taking account of pupils' views is largely dependent on commitment from school management. Wade and Moore's (1993) research on pupil participation from the perspective of head teachers needs to be treated with caution: only 67 heads were sampled. However, their findings are quite surprising. Around 50 per cent of heads rejected consultation with pupils on the grounds that it was 'time consuming, irrelevant and valueless' (1993, p. 45). Given that the researchers expected the heads to overestimate their commitment to pupils' rights, the figure in reality may be higher. These comments seem to strengthen the general view held by those with some influence in schools that children are positioned in relation to the formal structures of the school as incompetent.

In chapter 2 we saw how children were implicated in the policy network of responsibility and accountability through the 1989 Children Act. In child-care terms children became accountable agents. In terms of consumerism and the market-place there is little evidence that parents or educationalists are any more responsive to children. Nevertheless, there may be grounds for thinking that evidence of childhood agency is more likely to be found if we were to look at modes of accountability *inside* schools. Children have no formal voice within the market-place, yet they are clearly central as recipients of the curriculum and the actions of teachers. As I outlined in chapter 2, teachers have become more internally accountable through the kinds of disciplinary pressures exacted by the national curriculum. Thus, through the national curriculum and the greater prominence attached to pupil assessment, internal connections can be made between how well children are doing in class and the quality of teaching. What this suggests is that children's performances, both academic and behavioural, are more likely to have serious consequences for teachers than in previous educational regimes. The kinds of pressures that teachers are under to perform in school are now more directly related to the outcomes of formal pupil assessment. We might speculate here that children are more significant agents now in the way that they mediate a teacher culture. Two factors counter this possible trend. First, the national curriculum may give pupils a degree of leeway in that their academic performances through standard assessment tasks (SATS) have a more direct bearing on the teachers' professional sense of self. But as I have already argued (see p. 94), the formal channels for this pupil autonomy are absent. Teachers do not appear to be any more directly accountable to the pupils in class. There are no means by which pupils are able to voice an opinion on the quality of teaching or the content of the curriculum. Pupils' views and perceptions are at best interpreted by proxy, either through the kinds of demands placed on teachers to produce a new schooled version of childhood or through the parents as consumers. Second, pupils themselves are likely to be as constricted by the national curriculum as their teachers. Pollard's (1996, p. 120) research, for example, suggests that teachers are forced to modify the effects of the curriculum on primary school pupils by, among other things, holding on to more informal teaching methods in protecting pupils from the pressures of school assessment. Despite the centralizing effects of the national curriculum and associated assessments on the teaching profession, according to this research teachers still seem to have the upper hand in regulating the daily routine in primary classrooms.[4]

Curriculum and Pedagogy

Until now I have been arguing that, despite the shift towards more individualized forms of educational provision and organization, the education system has singularly failed to redefine the pupil as an active social agent. If we turn to the business of teaching and the introduction of a national curriculum, key educational actors – both young and old – are much more subject to centralized aims and objectives. Although there have been localized adult responses to the national curriculum in Britain in its original form, for example the selective boycotting of assessment and the recent reappraisal through the Dearing Report, the subject content of schooling is still largely determined at the political centre.

Proponents of the national curriculum have drawn on the language of rights in talking about an 'entitlements curriculum' (Barber, 1992; National Curriculum Council, 1992). The prenational curriculum period is characterized as a time when the 'core' subjects such as maths and science were not taught in any consistent way and lacked any depth. It was argued that a national curriculum would entitle children to similar educational experiences across the country and thus standardize the allegedly rather patchy coverage of some subjects. Clearly, there is some merit in widening pupil access to the more highly valued core subjects, particularly for groups of students who have been traditionally academically marginalized. To illustrate this point, a recent Equal Opportunities Commission report contends that the national curriculum is having some effect in narrowing the 'gender gap' between male and female take-up of subjects, particularly at GCSE level (Arnot, David and Weiner, 1996). Yet the national curriculum may prove to be too inflexible for some groups of students. One such group, non-statemented students with special educational needs (SEN), may have difficulty in dealing with the compulsory core and foundation subjects.[5] There is also an emphasis on English as the medium of communication in teaching and assessment. This may, in effect, compromise the entitlement to a broad-based curriculum for children whose home language is not English. Some critics have also hinted that the standardization of the curriculum has also meant that a particular kind of curriculum, one that broadly speaking reflects white metropolitan values, is imposed on a culturally diverse school population. An emphasis on 'Britishness' and on tradition in literature, history and music, rather than generate a common educational experience, might exacerbate existing social and cultural divisions in some English and Welsh schools (Hardy and Vieler-Porter, 1990; Ball, 1994). There may be groups of students who, for whatever reason, have difficulties with the national curriculum and have no means of redress.

Furthermore, the national curriculum within the broader context of a quasi-market in education weakens any notion of a child's entitlement rights. The introduction of league tables for academic performance and school attendance strengthens the positions of some schools at the cost of others. In their desire to attract parental preferences, schools are less likely to want to hold on to pupils with social and learning difficulties, students who are more likely to weaken a school's exam and attendance ratings. Pupils in these categories would appear to have fewer 'entitlement' rights than other pupils if we refer to market pressures on head teachers to present their schools in the best possible light to prospective adult consumers.

Although the national curriculum does not appear to offer all children equal access to educational goods, one group of pupils, those formally designated as having special needs, have gained some formal recognition with regard to childhood agency. Interestingly, this seems to be the only area within the broad spectrum of education reform in England and Wales where pupils' views are explicitly acknowledged. The 1994 Code of Practice on Identification and Assessment of Special Educational

Needs obliges teachers and educational psychologists to take account of the pupils' views during assessments. Reference is made to both the practical benefits of and the principled approach to children's involvement, with the former linked to the necessity of children's support for the 'effective implementation of individual education programmes' (2.35) and the latter referring to children's right to be heard.

In theory, children are to be consulted as part of the statementing process. A recent Ofsted report on the implementation of the Code of Practice states that these child-centred principles have yet to be systematically put into practice. Given that the schools, 62 from across England, were inspected just after the document had been published, we may be forgiven for thinking that a second visit several years later might elicit different and more positive results.[6] Recent research in this field by Armstrong and Galloway (1996) and Owen and Tarr (1998) indicates that it is doubtful whether the code of practice could ever work effectively in the child's interests. They argue that the process of consulting pupils and the whole structure of dialogue between client and professional serves to dis-able the role of the child client. First, the idea of being 'in need' implies a passive model of the client child, someone being acted upon and rendered dependent by professionals. The assessment presupposes that there is a problem and that the child's views are sought as part of the diagnosis. This makes it more difficult for the child to question whether there is any need for the assessment and challenge the imputed label of 'in need'. Armstrong and Galloway's (1996) interviews with pupils who had been formally assessed reveal that some pupils construed the assessment as a form of unwarranted intervention or punishment. Yet the pupils were powerless to make their views count because they were outside the professionals' terms of reference. In other words, children's views were to count once they accepted the need for an assessment. Second, even where child clients accepted these terms, few systematic attempts were made by professionals to involve them in the process and they had real difficulties in making sense of decisions taken as a result of their assessment (Armstrong and Galloway, 1996).

A final point rests on the position of SEN children, who seem to be doubly disadvantaged because of their imputed disabilities and their status as children. The researchers report that, where the child clients' views were sought, they were frequently dismissed on the grounds of incompetence: either because of imputed levels of cognition which, according to the professionals, rendered any children's statements less valid; or through the 'best interests' clause, whereby professionals speak on behalf of children of what they know to be in their own best interests. In sum: the absence of any pupil voice suggests that the entitlement curriculum is, at best, limited to the provision of an adequate education. It is up to the adult population, parents or inspectors, to register any formal opinion on the quality of this provision. To reiterate: pupils are unable to formally complain about the form and content of their schooling.

One set of educational principles that has historically been associated with pupil and teacher autonomy is the philosophy of child-centredness. As sociological researchers have found in classrooms, the notion of child-centredness is a highly contested set of pedagogic propositions which, when applied, are both enabling and constraining in their consequences for pupils. Entwistle (1974, p. 16), in a positive vein, claims that child-centredness means that 'the child is the agent of his [*sic*] own education'. On this basis, teacher time and school resources should be invested in creating autonomous spaces for children to work through their own curricula in their own ways. Child-centredness is also supposed to emphasize the teacher as a facilitator rather than someone who imposes the curriculum in class. Teachers are to monitor and survey rather than intervene in the child's learning process (Walkerdine, 1983).

If we turn to more negative interpretations, Sharp and Green (1975), for instance, argue that child-centredness has more rhetorical than philosophical or political power. The overriding priority for teachers here, particularly those working in deprived areas, is to maintain order. Any notion that the child takes control of the education process is interpreted by teachers in terms of the notion of 'busyness'. In effect, this means that the majority of less academically gifted pupils are left to their own devices so long as they keep themselves occupied. This is not the place to evaluate these conflicting interpretations of child-centredness. But it would be fair to say that a curricular shift to centrally determined academic standards, allied to the regular testing of pupils in a competitive environment, makes it very difficult to think that teachers are in a position to meet the particular academic interests of individual pupils or particular groups of pupils. There are also fewer grounds for thinking that teachers can underwrite the less conventional talents that the individual children might have through prolonged involvement and understanding of their emotional and social backgrounds.

As I discussed in chapter 2, child-centredness has been used as a reference point for a public critique of teaching styles, particularly in primary schools. A British government report asserted that the philosophy of child-centredness and its application has concentrated too much on 'individual discovery' and 'creative work' at the cost of prescribing subjects in a more didactic fashion (Alexander et al., 1992). There are two quite different implications here. First, the focus on play, on topic and group work and the spontaneous, some would say disorganized, nature of classroom dynamics allows the possibility that pupils themselves are able to take a degree of initiative in class (Jeffs, 1995, p. 29). This has been curtailed. Teachers are encouraged to return to centre-stage in the classroom and tackle the national curriculum in whole-class terms. Teacher-centredness has now become the order of the day, if not always in practice, certainly as official purpose. It thus becomes difficult to conceive of primary school pupils being able to structure their own learning or take the initiative in class. A second set of implications is rather more supportive of the national curriculum and brings us back to the idea of a pupil's entitlement. An over-emphasis on a non-intrusive 'facilitative' approach which stresses the more subtle adult policing of children's cognitive development may actually deprive pupils of knowledge. Children are to develop capacities rather than know things. As Berry Mayall puts it, 'the net effect of Piagetian [child-centred] teaching has been to devalue what children know; and thence their competence' (1996, p. 45). Rather ironically, a more teacher- or subject-centred approach, for all its deterministic outcomes for pupils, is one way of ensuring that children are exposed to a range of ideas and curricular material.

Schooling and Community

Problems of truancy and school exclusion have focused public attention on the relationship between school and community. In particular, a variety of strategies of control have been initiated to regulate public spaces around schools and protect members of the community from the alleged criminal effects of children's absences from school. Truancy watch schemes abound in shopping centres with the aim of identifying children 'out of place' (Paterson, 1989). Closed circuit television cameras are installed in schools and security consultants are employed by head teachers to deal with the perceived rise of violence in schools (*The Times*, 28 December 1995, p. 6). What we have here is the reaffirming of the adult imperative of control which was discussed earlier with reference to the problems of child protection and child crime. In dealing with youthful violence and children on the street, schools have been drawn into an ever-expanding network of regulation and control.

If we turn to the analysis of one form of school absence, truancy, the largest and most recent survey in England and Wales takes a child-centred line. This is surprising given that the author, Denis O'Keeffe (1994), is a contributor to the Institute of Economic Affairs (IEA), a prominent right-wing think-tank. In treating pupils as economic actors,

O'Keeffe argues that children vote with their feet in staying away from school. He depicts the school and classroom as a market-place where pupils exchange compliance for enjoyment, knowledge and qualifications. This exchange, according to the author, has now broken down, with pupils both staying away from school (blanket truancy) and avoiding certain lessons (post-registration truancy) because school offers no perceptible pay-off. O'Keeffe goes on to suggest that post-registration truancy is more popular than blanket truancy because pupils adopt a cost–benefit approach in avoiding certain less popular, less well taught or less relevant subjects like English, Physical Education and French. He is thus cautious about inferring any rejection of school *per se* from his data. Of those who claimed to have truanted at least once a term (around 30 per cent of the sample) less than half (49 per cent) rejected school outright.

O'Keeffe also seems to acknowledge a degree of childhood rationality here. He is careful to differentiate peer-related reasons for truancy, with their connotations of children being herd-like and instinctive in being led astray, from more rational grounds. He argues that 'truancy is largely a social phenomenon, but one based on individual choice . . . peer pressure and bullying are influences but only small ones. Truancy though largely social in character is a voluntary act' (1994, p. 62). Truants are thus treated as competent actors in the way that they make judgements about whether or not certain lessons are worth attending. Although there is nothing explicit in O'Keeffe's report recommending a fully blown 'children's rights' approach to compulsory education, we might speculate that by treating children as economic actors there is a degree of legitimacy accorded to children who rationally decide to avoid school. This report proposes that, as rational agents, children are capable of making decisions that affect their immediate and long-term goals. Logically, any notion of the child as an active participant or a self-determining agent implied by this report gives the child the right to choose not to go to school. We need to be careful not to draw too many 'child-centred' conclusions from this research. O'Keeffe's prescriptions rest on an increase in a variety of forms of adult vigilance. There is also a degee of pathologizing the problem of truancy by shifting from blaming parents to targeting the alleged inadequacies of schools and teachers. Still, if we follow the logic of this argument, the compulsory nature of schooling is being questioned along the lines of more 'liberationist'-type approaches (cf. Jeffs, 1995).

More recent analysis and policy prescriptions follow the orthodoxy in arguing that education is a public good that should be enjoyed by all children. Any idea that policy makers are likely to tinker around with the compulsory nature of schooling is firmly and formally rejected in a recent Labour government report published by the Social Exclusion Unit which states that, '[I]n the long run, the objective must be to ensure that education ceases to be optional' (1998, p. 2). As well as truancy, the report also focuses on school exclusion, the formal expulsion of children from school. In one sense, school exclusion contradicts the compulsory nature of schooling and any notion that children have an entitlement to education. It is important to stress that school exclusion disproportionately affects some groups of pupils rather than others. Gillborn (1996), in his study of ethnic minority pupils and school achievement, confirms the point. Between four and six times as many Afro-Caribbean as 'white' pupils are excluded from school. The Social Exclusion Unit does take issue with the 'profligate' use of school exclusion but, as with SEN pupils, the educational market generates counter-pressures on heads to exclude 'difficult' children.

The Social Exclusion Unit report clearly expresses concern for the child's present and future well-being, with a commitment to schooling as a necessary if sometimes pragmatic means of improving life chances. Yet this policy document also has to be taken as part of the broader context of control discussed earlier. There is the perennial connection made between lost schooldays and the problems of crime and delinquency. The links are most explicit in the recent Crime and Disorder Act (1998) whereby police have increased powers to remove from public places children who appear to be truanting. Whilst policy makers are apt to confuse a correlation with a causal factor, the 'correlation' is effective in drawing heads, teachers and parents into a nexus of blame and control (Carlen, Gleeson and Wardhaugh, 1992, p. 155). Truancy and school exclusion as forms of problems seem to follow the general policy direction in making adults – teachers and parents – more responsible for children's misdemeanours out of school hours and away from the radius of the home. We referred in chapter 2 to the way that child policy has been heavily influenced by a culture of blame, with a consequent focus on more individualized adult strategies of control. This is well illustrated if we refer back to another policy document, the Education White Paper where a key cornerstone of the British government's education policy is to try and strengthen relations between home and school through the notion of home–school contracts (DfEE, 1997, p. 55).

What is interesting here is that children themselves appear to play no part in these new networks of control. Again, we cannot help but point to the stark contrast between child-care and education settings. Children's opinions are now more likely to be heard in child-care cases, giving them more say in any changes to their domestic circumstances.

Home–school contracts, on the other hand, seem to be attempts to regulate children's behaviour on the ground 'at a distance' by committing
parents and teachers to written agreements which make both parties
responsible for the child's behaviour in school. There is, importantly
here, no reference to trilateral relations between parent, child and school.
Home–school contracts are explicitly bilateral involving parents and
teachers where courses of action on the pupil's welfare are agreed between
consenting adults.

Conclusion

Recent changes within the education system stemming from government legislation have affected almost all aspects of a child's education.
The transformation of the form and content of schooling and relations
between school and community have not taken consistent directions in
relation to the binary division between state and individual. The stated
aim of making the education system more accountable to the individual
consumer does not sit easily with the imposition of a centrally determined national curriculum. However, as I argued in chapter 2, although
education takes the child population as its primary object of concern,
with the exception of one or two areas such as special educational needs,
the child does not figure within these changes as an active social agent.
He or she is excluded from changes that are tending to work at the local
as well as national and global levels. The targeting of governing bodies,
head teachers and most significantly parents in terms of their 'individual'
capacities may have variable effects. In some instances parents, probably
the more affluent ones, have had their roles enhanced as consumers (Ball,
Bowe and Gewirtz, 1995). At the same time heads and governors from
the better placed schools have had their positions strengthened through
the freeing up of school rolls. But the great majority of professionals and
'consumers' become more deeply implicated within a culture of blame
and control which puts them under more pressure to account for their
child work.

What may be more significant from the pupils' perspective is a greater
sense of exploitation. We can refer to the formal absence of the child from
any involvement in the localizing of education decision-making. We
can allude to the marginalized position of pupils at the school and community level of decision-making. We might also add to this the way in
which policy is intensifying the work that children do through an
increase in classroom assessment and a much stronger emphasis on
schoolwork that children do at home. In one sense, the government's
recent homework policy as featured in the 1997 White Paper reflects the

need to regulate and control children's time and space in the pursuit of 'economic prosperity and social justice' (1997, p. 1). Parents may become more tied to the school indirectly through policies that promote joint educational ventures which strengthen the government's commitment to the testing of children at ever younger ages and through contractual obligations over children's homework and out-of-school behaviour. This inevitably leads to restrictions on the child's time and the attenuation of space for child's play. Drawing on Oldman's theory, we might speculate that the intensification of 'child work' has led to the intensification of children's work (1994) which has little to do with empowering children in schools. We might take the view that education reform is an attempt to standardize children's experiences and thus treat children simply as another social grouping that can be brought into line along with other groups in society. Interestingly, we have the convergence of crisis and reconstructionist accounts of childhood discussed in chapter 1. We could say that the institution of childhood is compromised as children have fewer opportunities to play and act out their 'childish' instincts. We might also speculate that viewing children as members of a minority group allows us to identify the different ways in which education further exploits children. Regardless of the line that we take here, education policy clearly defines children as ontologically absent in social and political terms. Adults take up education for children and are accountable to other adults for the educational services they provide. Paraphrasing Armstrong and Galloway (1996, p. 111), education policy clearly demonstrates that children are still the property of adults.

5 Childhood and Citizenship

Introduction

In chapter 4 I argued that education reform seems to reduce the possibility for pupils to participate in and have some sort of control over their education. Although there are clearly possibilities for other local agencies, namely parents and head teachers, schools have become steadfastly more bureaucratic and more adult-centred through the need to measure output and regulate the internal and external activities of schoolchildren. Although I framed the analysis in terms of childhood and agency by viewing children as members of a minority group, this is not confirmed within an educational context. The rights and responsibilities of children, either as members of a social group or individually, are largely absent from recent education reform. There is therefore little consideration of their having any rights to participate or to be heard collectively. In this chapter I want to view the education policy domain differently. I address educational developments in and around the grand educational narratives associated with education reform such as organization, curriculum and assessment, which may bring us closer to the idea of children as social agents. In the concluding section of the chapter I pursue in more detail a comparison between the positions of children discussed in this and the previous chapter. At this stage I merely want to comment that, through a combination of pragmatism, innovation and on occasion necessity, we can identify some possibilities within schools for children as social agents.

In this chapter agency is understood partly in terms of social ontology, but more specifically in terms of the concept of citizenship. I examine a series of relatively recent educational initiatives that take us a little closer to viewing children as a minority group within society which makes claims on them as citizens. The notion of citizenship is a status bestowed on members of society on the basis of the kinds of skills and abilities that are traditionally associated with adulthood. Moreover, this is explicitly acknowledged with reference to a series of rights that adults have, ranging from rights to information and participation through to rights to economic support. This chapter makes no claims to viewing children in these terms. Nevertheless, a limited view of citizenship might be demonstrated through the incorporation of children into the adult world of information and knowledge; it might be viewed in terms of a degree of participation. Finally, the 'child as citizen' theme might imply the more modest notion that children have a degree of social, moral and political competence. With reference to the 'child as citizen' theme then, I first of all outline the introduction of peer support networks in primary schools. I include here material from research that I carried out in this field. The material will be drawn on for illustrative purposes only. Second, I go on to examine changes to the national curriculum, namely the intoduction of sex education, which has some potential for incorporating children within the adult world of morality and sexuality. An analysis of sex education is followed by an examination of recent debates on the teaching of citizenship. In particular, I summarize the key elements of a government report on citizenship education within the national curriculum. Although this document sets out an innovative approach to children's relations within the political world, the political representation of children is one subject conspicuously absent. In the final part of the chapter I address this omission with reference to the role of child advocates.

Children as Peacemakers

To illustrate the possibilities of childhood competence, I want to turn to localized initiatives set up to encourage 'pro-social' behaviour in schools. In Britain, North America and parts of Europe peer support networks have become increasingly popular in encouraging children, particularly children within primary schools, to become more active in regulating their own and their peers' behaviour. These peer networks have taken a variety of forms. Helen Cowie and her colleagues (1996) discuss the emergence of these pro-social skills in class through the introduction of peer support services in nine secondary and primary schools in south-east England. Their research was based on a variety of forms of peer support from 'buddy' or befriending services between pupils to mediation and counselling support, where specific conflicts between pupils in school are dealt with by pupils trained in conflict resolution. More recently, secondary school pupils from 80 schools within the Manchester area are being trained to act as student counsellors. With funding from Childline and the support of the University of Manchester, the schools are opening up drop-in centres where pupils can consult with peer counsellors on a range of problems from family bereavements to bullying (*The Times*, 5 February 1998, p. 8).

If we look more specifically at the idea of peer mediation, we find children demonstrating many of the classic mediation skills found at community, national and international levels. Mediation is an established method of bringing warring factions together. In recent years mediation has been applied to marital disputes, neighbourhood conflict and industrial action. Primary schools within several regions of the United Kingdom are training children as young as 7 to take more responsibility for policing behaviour within the playground. My own involvement is in monitoring the introduction of peer mediation in primary and secondary schools within central England.[1] The pupils known to the other children as peer mediators are 'on duty' during break times and can normally be found within certain designated areas of the playground. Although more and more serious incidents are being dealt with by the mediators themselves, violent behaviour and incidents of an overtly racist nature tend to be dealt with by the teaching staff. Peer mediators in most cases are expected to intercede where there are low-level disputes such as name calling, general verbal disagreements and threatening behaviour between pupils. Mediators can also be approached by pupils themselves and asked to help with a range of problems. In most cases the following scenario takes place. The mediator will identify problems or be called on to separate the disputants. This is usually followed by a 'cooling-off' period where the parties involved are encouraged to approach the peer mediators after a period of time and talk through their problems. Peer mediators take on a counselling type of role which involves working together with the opposing factions in an effort to encourage them to talk through their disagreements. A typical scenario would be for four pupils to sit in pairs opposite each other. The disputants face each other whilst the peer mediators help them to work through their problems. The mediators set out the rules of the interaction. The disputants in turn are given some time to put forward their version of events without interruption. The mediators will try and get them to come to some agreement or, at the very least, get them on speaking terms. An important principle which the mediators have to follow is the need to work through the disputants' problems without passing judgement or imputing blame.

From a psychological perspective various authors refer to the advantages that peer mediation has for the child's personal growth and development (Adalbjarnardottir, 1994; Stacey and Robinson, 1996;

Cowie and Sharp, 1996). Although the strengthening of self-esteem and the process of decentring are important, I want to pick up here on the specific social advantages that peer mediation has for pupils as part of a minority social group. In other words, I am interested in how mediation develops children's skills of conflict resolution in social settings. I am also interested in the way that schools which introduce peer mediation already seem to assume that children have a degree of social competence. In the following section I address the currency of peer mediation, its potential for tackling a range of child-oriented issues as well as its limitations at peer, school and macro levels.

Peer Level

Children are better equipped than adults to deal with conflict between pupils for the simple reason that they are more knowledgeable about what goes on in the playground. They are more likely to confide in their peers than in their teachers that they are being bullied. Children are keenly aware of the dynamics of their peer groups and very conscious of situations that are likely to erupt into conflict (Hale, Farley-Lucas and Tardy, 1996). Importantly, children are deeply implicated in what Cullingford calls the 'volatile "underworld"' of schooling (1993, p. 58). They have a much more acute sense of what constitutes 'abnormal' or 'abusive' aggression in school than the teachers. Pragmatically, then, peer mediation is an effective means of dealing with peer conflict. Now at the phenomenological level this might bring children into conflict with teachers. In her ethnography of children's playground activities, Thorne (1993) reflects on her own observations of children playing which brought to the fore a tension between the adult's need to protect children from physical encounters and the normal rough and tumble of children's interactions within the playground. As an adult, researcher and mother, Thorne was trying to adjust her viewpoint to the possibility that physical contact was an integral part of peer-group interaction. At the formal structural level, peer mediation – by granting children a degree of autonomy in defining problems between peers – potentially avoids these kinds of disagreements. Problems, then, particularly those construed as threatening or abusive, are defined as such by those most affected by them, the pupils.

In a broader sense peer mediation is supposed to work on improving the child's co-operative skills and values such as listening, understanding and tolerance. Sonia Sharp (1996) refers in her review of peer support networks to the way skills are enhanced by schools adopting management techniques from industry such as 'Quality Circle Time'. In most schools circle time is introduced at the preliminary stage of mediation training as a way of developing a co-operative ethic in schools. Children are encouraged to express an opinion and are expected to listen, to understand and tolerate the views of others. It thus potentially prepares all children for the role of mediator.

School Level

Peer mediation is said to strengthen existing pedagogic principles of individual development 'within context' by reinforcing school values such as tolerance, understanding and personal self-worth. It also offers more radical challenges to dominant school values of individualism and adult responsibility. Peer mediation becomes part of what has been termed a 'whole school' philosophy which directly confronts these values. It replaces the emphasis on individual achievement through competitive endeavour with stronger notions of school and classroom co-operation. This is not simply a question of strengthening the classroom as the means to greater individual success, but of generating more collective ways of solving problems. Peer mediation also has the potential to distribute school responsibility and education ownership more evenly across the school, incorporating the idea of the responsible child in terms of both rights and obligations (see chapter 2). As Stacey and Robinson say in their recent text on conflict resolution, 'peer mediation gives pupils ownership of their resolution of disputes' (1996, p. 8). Pupils rather than adults provide the social support needed by peers who are having difficulty in integrating or who are experiencing more long-term problems such as victimization and racism (Cowie et al., 1996). Problems of control and pupil self-esteem become part of a range of issues examined at the school level. In theory, this means that all school members are committed to a process of self-evaluation and change. Pupils as well as teachers, heads and governors are involved in policy making based on the principles of co-operation.

'Macro' Level

The advantages for children of peer mediation at the macro level are not so immediately obvious. As with the idea of the child as a reliable witness outlined in chapter 3, there is no clear child-centred policy agenda here. On the one hand, peer mediation is part of a broader European project to promote 'pro-social' behaviour in schools (see Moreno and Torrego, 1998). The context here is 'anti-social behaviour [which is] perceived to be a growing source of trouble in European school systems' (ibid. p. 2). The aim of this project is to change underlying attitudes across the school by, among other things, altering the curriculum, reviewing pedagogic practice and discipline management in classrooms and introducing 'methods of democratic conflict resolution' (ibid., p. 9). Yet the democratizing of the classroom is not the sole rationale for the take-up of this initiative by politicians, educators and to some extent by teachers themselves. Peer support networks have received considerable media attention over the past few years, partly because of the perceived increase in aggression in schools (Platt, 1994). Bullying is part of the broader agenda of control in schools. This has in turn led to a tightening of disciplinary mechanisms which restricts rather than enhances pupils' autonomy in school.

There are elements of this in the government's White Paper on education (DfEE, 1997, p. 56). Schools are expected to integrate 'localised initiatives' with 'assertive discipline', which is taken by government as a model of good practice. Schools which have adopted this approach have imposed a framework of rules 'emphasising positive encouragement as well as clear sanctions' (p. 56). There are two ways of interpreting the policy here. First, peer mediation as the localized initiative becomes a 'child-centred' appendage to more conventional adult-oriented approaches, where teachers and heads clearly set the disciplinary agenda. We have here a mix of more traditional methods of discipline and, within certain very limited contexts, children themselves *applying* school rules. Second, and more cynically, peer mediation becomes a radical quick fix for a media-induced panic over violence in schools. Peer mediation is therefore adopted where the more conventional adult-centred approaches have been exhausted. There may be situations where peer mediation is adopted by schools in specific year groups or classes where bullying is perceived to be at its worst and where peer mediation becomes one in a long line of possible 'solutions'.

Dan Olweus' (1995) work in Norway focuses on the introduction of anti-bully charters where children and teaching staff put together school strategies for dealing with aggression in school. Peer support networks thus get built in to what are termed 'whole school approaches'. In several of my research schools, a whole school approach did pretty much amount to a series of 'bottom-up' decisions, where pupils were more instrumental in putting together school discipline policies that placed an emphasis on pupil participation and regulation. Some authors, though, have been sceptical of the way in which whole school policies have been used by head teachers as a form of window dressing to conceal the less than democratic nature of policy making in school (Hawtin and Wise, 1997). This can be seen in schools where decisions on the adoption of peer mediation, for example, are often taken by the teaching staff, with little or no pupil consultation. We are in the rather ironic situation here that peer mediation is introduced into some schools by head teachers as a radical pupil-centred initiative without any explicit support from the pupils themselves.

One limitation of peer mediation rests on the theoretical distinction referred to in chapters 1 and 4 between the 'tribal' and 'social structural' child (James, Jenks and Prout, 1998). Although I am hinting in this chapter that certain kinds of educational initiatives could have real benefits for children as a social group within the wider society, there is a tendency to think of peer mediation in terms of the tribal child. The crux of peer mediation is the co-operative, collective nature of being in the world. We could say that as children mediate within the playground, this world is primarily restricted to children. Children, as it were, police their own. If we refer to the primary data, peer mediators themselves were aware of this when discussing their responsibilities. During the group interview with the peer mediators, references were made to the restrictions placed on their roles as mediators.

Tara (aged 11):   If someone's got a problem outside of . . . friendship problems, they can't come to us, they have to go to a senior member of staff. I don't like that. I think mediators should be able to give some sort of advice – if the problem's that big . . . As mediators we should be able to do something about those problems as well . . .

Interviewer: So it's because of problems that you can't help with, that's what you don't like . . .?
Yes (general agreement).

Tara: Yes . . . problems like smoking, breaking school rules . . . We've got quite a big school something like 1600 pupils in our school . . . counting the sixth form. That's a big school: lots of problems.

Mary (aged 14):   At school X, we do counselling as well . . . Hm . . . We've got a rule that if we've got a big problem, we're always there to listen . . . And that's an important part of mediation . . . So if there's something wrong and we can't do this and we can't do that, we're just there to listen. And that helps.

This extract illustrates one of the dilemmas facing peer mediators. Once trained, the mediators were motivated to help others. They took for granted their roles as advisors and counsellors and mediation became part of their school routine. They couldn't quite come to terms with the way that the school had encouraged them to befriend and support their peers but at the same time place restrictions on the kinds of problems that they could handle.

Peer mediation might on the surface appear tokenistic in that children are limited to specific problems within marginal educational areas such as the child-dominated confines of the playground. Yet peer mediation is more than this. First, disagreements between pupils do not always originate in the playground – mediators often deal with classroom-based conflicts that spill over into the playground. Second, if we view mediation as part of a process, playground conflicts move swiftly into the more socially established adult-controlled space of the classroom, tutorial room and office. Peer mediation, with its patterns of child responsibility, forces children into these adult realms. The above extract exemplifies the 'structural' potential for peer mediation, for pupils are aware of the limits of what probably seem to be arbitrary boundaries between serious and less important issues. Furthermore, the children interviewed were from different schools and attended the conference in order to discuss and compare mediating experiences. If we refer to the extract, there is a clear sense in which the comparison of mediators' experiences rests on some schools allowing their mediators more latitude than other schools. There is thus no hard and fast rule as to how much pupils can mediate.

Regardless of its marginal status in some schools, peer mediation can challenge an essentially adult function, the discipline and control of children. Teachers have the authority to define and regulate bad behaviour. The convention holds – one that is central to the crisis thesis discussed in chapter 1 – that discipline is a principal means for keeping children in line and reinforcing their subordinate position within the social structure. In terms of routine disciplinary practices in school, peer mediation is an application which highlights the 'agentic' role of children within the adult world. Thus, whether peer mediation is an adult-inspired initiative imposed on schoolchildren, the ongoing practice of children working through a range of problems on their own creates more ambiguous relations between adults and children.

The crossing of the adult–child status boundary, interestingly, is an issue the peer mediators themselves are only too aware of. If we return to Mary, the mediator with more adult-type responsibilities, she refers to the status boundary between pupil and teacher.

> I don't know about any other mediators, but I feel . . . I wouldn't be able to mediate a teacher because of the authority that teachers have

over us . . . I mean . . . faced with a situation with a pupil and
teacher . . . I wouldn't know how to react . . . If a teacher was sitting
in front of you – they could say just one thing . . . It's difficult to
mediate a teacher.

(Mary)

Mary is aware of the possibilities, not to say the logic, of peer mediation
as a whole school practice in the way that she is able to consider the difficulties of applying mediation to pupil–teacher relations. The fact that
she has to consider the possibility of mediating a teacher may be related
to the earlier point that she has a wider set of mediating responsibilities.
It may also be linked to the dilemma discussed earlier over how to limit
areas for mediation. The limits are not simply defined in terms of the
kinds of activities, but potentially in terms of the kinds of people who
can be mediated. Mary was able to intercede in more serious issues like
bullying which might bring her into conflict with the teachers' conventional disciplinary roles. The point I want to make here is that peer
mediation, at least for this pupil, involves a degree of renegotiation of her
school position, with the potential for her to become more active within
the adult world of boundaries and rules.

The ambiguities over mediator–teacher relations can also be found
with respect to relations that peer mediators have with their peers. Mary
goes on to identify the significance of the status boundary in terms of the
ambiguous relationship she has with her friends.

I think though . . . becoming a mediator . . . it's different than in
primary school. I used to hang around in gangs . . . I think now in
some situations, I feel like an outsider with my friends . . . They're
talking about, you know, bashing somebody up, you know, arguing
or something, or just talking. But I'm a mediator, so it's different
now . . . They can't tell everything to me . . . because they think I'll
go and tell the teacher.

There is some ambivalence expressed here which seems to be reflected in
the perceptions that the larger sample of mediators have of their new
roles within school. In referring to Table 1 we need to be very careful
when extrapolating from these figures for there are clear differences
between primary and secondary responses.[2] Nevertheless, a majority of
pupils could see the benefits of their work for themselves and their peers:
overall 81 per cent expressed more satisfaction with school and 86 per
cent of mediators were of the opinion that peer mediation was working
as a means of reducing conflict. Again, we need to be cautious: although

Table 1 Pupil responses to peer mediation questions (from 20 questions)[1]

Question	Primary		Secondary		Totals (%)	
	Yes	No	Yes	No	Yes	No
6. Do your friends like you being a mediator?	40	39	10	19	46	54
10. Are there fewer quarrels at school now that you are a mediator?	74	5	1	28	86	14
12. Are you better at lessons now that you are a mediator?	45	34	13	16	54	45
13. Are you happier at school now that you are a mediator?	76	3	11	18	81	19

Source: Silcock, Stacey and Wyness (1996).

Note 1: n = 108.

the sample size of secondary and primary school pupils is, strictly speaking, not comparable, the 'happiness' quotient was much higher in primary than secondary schools. This difference is brought out in question 6, which assesses relations with peers. If we take the sample as a whole, more than half thought that being a peer mediator had a negative effect on their friendships with peers. Children enjoy the challenge of their new roles but have problems in negotiating their new status with their peers and teachers.

Peer mediation, because it bestows on the child a degree of ownership over the education process, assumes that children are socially competent. An important dimension of childhood agency is a belief that children are skilled social actors in a range of quite diverse settings. The conventional education project takes a developmental line in the way that it refines the points of entry children have into the adult world. These points of entry are determined by theories of learning and cognition but they are also shaped by the impetus to protect, particularly in the case of primary school pupils. The work of Epstein (1993) is instructive. In her research on infant schools she examines the notion that very young children

cannot be given routine responsibilities in school for their own social and
emotional well-being because they do not have the requisite cognitive or
social skills. She argues that this incompetence tends to be articulated
through the idea of childhood innocence whereby young children
embody an earlier pre-social stage close to nature. This innocence and
incompetence is played out routinely in the way that teachers tend to
ignore children's 'racist' comments because children are unable to comprehend that they are causing harm.

As I outlined in chapter 3, social competence is supposed to come with
age and experience. It develops almost in inverse proportion to the child's
innocence. The segregation of children from routine social activities
which might demand a more active and formative involvement is a way
of sustaining this notion of innocence. I will say more about the ideology
of innocence later. What can be said here is that peer mediation contradicts or at least softens the idea that children are innocents unable to play
a full role within society. We have seen how this contradiction affects
children themselves through the ambivalence expressed over their relations with friends. This ambivalence is also felt by some practitioners
who, although committed to child-centred initiatives, are uncertain
about the abilities of very young children. One head teacher of an infant
school which had introduced peer mediation a year earlier, expresses her
misgivings in terms of notions of competence and innocence: 'I did not
expect children of 6 or 7 years to be able to deal with race and bullying
problems. Indeed I wondered if I was putting too much responsibility on
them at the beginning' (head teacher, infant school, Birmingham). This
quote illustrates the tension between the children's own rights and
responsibilities and the teacher's need to protect and nurture to a state of
readiness.

Sex Education and the Informed Child

In chapter 1 I discussed the alleged disappearance of childhood among
modern western children, namely the notions of innocence, cuteness and
naïvety. Children are innocent because they are excluded from the world
of knowledge. If we return to Postman's thesis, the essence of childhood
is the existence of secrets: 'children are curious because they do not yet
know what they suspect there is to know' (1982, p. 89). They lose their
innocence because they become implicated in a new technology of
knowledge that exposes them to an ever-expanding world of images and
information which in turn generates demands on behalf of children and
arguably from children for more knowledge. Others of a liberationist
bent have responded by asserting that this knowledge is still limited to

what we as adults think children should know; and that the tendency is still for children to be exposed gradually to a sanitized and highly structured body of knowledge (Holt, 1975; Farson, 1978). They argue that this sustains one of the key ideological structures of childhood, the relative ignorance of children. The exclusion of children from the public sphere thus is seen to be arbitrary and unjustifiable.

In this book I have been trying to mark out a midpoint between these two positions. As I discussed in chapter 3, the exclusion of children is now more difficult to sustain because of the dangers inherent in leaving children in a state of 'blissful' ignorance. I referred to the way in which the problem of child sexual abuse has generated political and institutional pressures for more informed children with the knowledge and skills to use in potentially abusive situations, and the acceptance of children as reliable witnesses. Sex education, particularly in Britain and the United States, is a useful starting point for an analysis of the informed child. This is because the demands for sex education have always been secondary to the need to retain children's innocence and their relative ignorance.

Before setting out the position in Britain, it is worth pointing to the situation in other countries. By way of illustration, in Australia sex education policy takes a 'libertarian' line. In their analysis of sex education at the state level in Australia, Lupton and Tulloch (1996, pp. 254–255) refer to libertarianism as the privileging of

> 'knowledge', incorporating both information and understanding, as the key to achieving responsible and fulfilling sexual expression . . . developing a heightened self-consciousness, a better understanding of the sexual self. They [the policy documents] represent sexuality as having the potential to be both 'satisfying' and 'creative' if properly understood.

Despite their argument that this policy does not always easily translate into practice, teachers have been encouraged to discuss a range of issues with children relating sex to, among other things, HIV and 'safer sex'. Since the 1970s there has been an openness around sexual issues and a requirement to keep pupils informed. Sex education policy in Britain, on other hand, has been more notable for its marked absence. The paucity of principled guidance on issues relating to the sexual realm is largely a consequence of the strictures of a set of values which links sex to socially sanctioned private relations between adults, what Lupton and Tulloch (1996) call a moral 'romanticism'. The advocacy of a curriculum that deals with all the ramifications of the sexual realm has until recently been met by a response that oscillates between indifference and moral outrage. This negative response reflects the notion that sex education in Britain seems to challenge the way educationalists think about the pupil population. It draws out many of the fears expressed within the public sphere: concerns about children's vulnerability, their alleged readiness to take part in civil society and their inability to safeguard their innocence. In short, the pro-sex education lobby in Britain directly confronts the ideology of innocence.

Since the early 1970s sex education has been a bone of contention within both educational and political spheres. In political terms there is the state–family opposition discussed in chapter 2. Issues around the provision of sex education have been framed in terms of a conflict between the rights of parents to educate their children in sexual matters and the collective interests of the state through the teaching profession to ensure that children are adequately instructed in these matters. The conflation of sex with morality and morality with privacy has focused attention on 'the family' as a realm of discretion. Parents are seen as the authority figures mediating between the increasingly complex public world of sexual congress and the child's alleged innate asocial nature.

A second conflict, one that cuts across state–family boundaries, is between adult authority as expressed through Postman's notion of 'secrets' and children's right to knowledge about their bodies. From a right-wing perspective generational tensions accentuate the interventionist role of the school. Teachers are accused of arrogating the rights of parents. The issue here is whether sex education denies parents a key moral duty, the guiding of children through the moral terrain of sexual relationships. This is articulated in terms of a shift in socializing functions from home to school and the extent to which this change threatens the moral order because teachers cannot be trusted to discuss the appropriate 'romanticized' values of chastity and fidelity. It is also arguably a threat for it signals the move from 'amateur' to professional spheres. The professionalization of morals has long been a concern of sociologists. Lasch (1977) and Popenoe (1988) have argued that sexual morals are rooted in the natural realm of family because of the biological and social responsibilities bestowed on parents. According to this line of argument, the influence of professionals can only be negative because they have the potential to mystify – technical knowledge within the sexual sphere is said to confuse students in their attempts to identify clear moral guidelines. There is also the possibility of suggestion. Teachers are accused of broaching the subject far too early in the child's career (cf. the repeal of CAPP in California, discussed in chapter 3). Children without the necessary moral infrastructure are more likely to experiment with sex before they are supposedly 'ready'. Sex education consequently becomes a means of calibrating innocence. Common sense – the realm of the 'amateur' – dictates intuitive points in the child's development for parents when their children are able to cope with the incremental acquisition of knowledge on sex.

More damagingly, teachers are seen to be state functionaries whose natural inclinations are to liberate children in generational and political terms. Sex education has thus been associated with the children's rights and anti-family movements of the early 1970s – the freeing of children from the 'tyranny' of family and adult control.[3] Sex education was also seen to be mixed up with the revolutionary fervour of 1960s radicalism, in which sexual politics became a metaphor for economic and political change. Radicals were not so much interested in abolishing childhood as in harnessing the revolutionary potential of young people in particular political directions. Sexual radicals and the allegedly insidious influence of a permissive culture are key factors in the opening up of the world of sex to children. This in turn has consequences for their positions within family and wider society.

Recent national and global events have produced more ambiguous lines of dissent. The developing AIDS crisis in the early 1980s produced a hysterical homophobia in which AIDS was framed in both medical and pseudo-religious terms as both a 'gay plague' and a form of retribution for 'unnatural' practices (Aggleton, 1988). This was reinforced by concerns over the teaching of homosexuality in sex education classes for the early years in London. Schools within the Haringey area of London were accused of normalizing homosexual relations by depicting gay couples with children in typical nuclear family situations. The media furore was followed by Clause 28, written into the Local Government Bill (1986), which proscribed the 'promotion' of homosexuality in schools.[4] A third feature of this homophobia is the pressures in the late 1980s to equalize the disparity between ages of consent for heterosexual (16) and homosexual (21) practices which were countered by what Johnson refers to as the extension of a 'childlike status' beyond the conventional age of 18 to incorporate the 'innocence' of young men between the ages of 16 and 21 (cited in Haywood, 1996, pp. 123–124).[5] The status of childhood is implicitly attached to 'vulnerable' 20-year-old men supposedly at risk from the predatory and promiscuous instincts of older homosexual men. Research within this area suggests that these issues have perplexed teachers and restricted the kinds of information they can draw on in giving children an accurate and balanced picture of sexual relations (Aggleton, 1988; Mac an Ghaill, 1994; Haywood 1996).

Whilst the general tenor of the anti-sex education lobby is to keep children within a state of relative ignorance, there is a degree of ambivalence in their criticisms of sex education in Britain. On the one hand, the reticence in dealing with the sexual development of the very young is a reflection of our need to protect the innocence of children. On the other hand, a rejection of sexual pluralism is reflected in the need to ensure that sexual matters are discussed with reference to heterosexuality and the nuclear family. There is thus a desire to broach the subject of legitimate sexual relationships. Other sexual orientations are either not discussed or marginalized as either deviant practices or medical conditions. These curricular constraints need to be set against the volume of literature and images that households and schools in Britain were bombarded with in the mid-1980s as the early homophobic period gave way to a more pandemic concern over heterosexual practices as well. Young people were now being exposed to more information on a range of different sexual practices in quite indiscriminate forms. Whether this period produced a more informed youth population is open to question.[6] What it did do was to extend the discourse on sexual practices into both public and private domains in such a way that it was becoming increasingly difficult to exclude children. Children are now more immersed in the formal and informal adult talk about sex. In previous research, for example, I have pointed out that terms such as 'condoms', which had previously been taboo, were now topics for humorous discussion between parents and children. To some extent 'sex talk' within the home had been 'normalized' (Wyness, 1996).

I have also referred to the pragmatic position taken by many teachers on sex education. Despite their personal or moral convictions, teachers tended to see the school as the most effective and, in some cases, exclusive forum for the discussion of ideas and problems relating to sexuality (Wyness, 1996a). Teachers were aware of the influence of the sexual discourse on pupils, conscious of the way information on sex can easily get distorted and thus felt compelled as professionals to regulate such information. This pragmatism can also be found in policy documents which referred to sex education. A major health initiative, the *Health of the Nation* (1992), commissioned by the Department of Health, sets out an agenda for halving the teenage pregnancy rate in Britain by the year 2000 through, among other things, encouraging schools to provide a more informed sex education curriculum. The report also advocates a national campaign to deal with the prevention of HIV. 'HIV Prevention Coordinators' are to be equipped to work with, among others, 'local education authority workers to develop HIV educational work in schools and colleges' (1992, p. 88). Sex education in this document is part of a project to promote healthier lifestyles, with 'older children' in particular being targeted.[7]

Despite its many limitations, the 1993 Education Act seems to follow this pragmatic line in taking a conditional pro-sex education position. The Act makes provision for sex education to be included in the national curriculum. Now compulsory sex education is limited to the secondary schools and there are restrictions on the content of what can be taught. The Act has not followed the advice of the *Health of the Nation*: AIDS and HIV have been excluded as compulsory topics for classroom discussion.[8] It is also important to set out the conditional nature of this curriculum, for the Act incorporates a parental veto. Parents have the final say over the child's sex education in that they can withdraw their children from sex education classes. As Hawtin and Wise (1997) acutely observe, the Act, in theory, produces the absurd situation whereby pupils can be denied access to certain types of information on sex two years after the age of heterosexual consent.

Having referred to these limitations, the government is for the first time legislating for the compulsory teaching of sex education. Sex education has to be provided for all pupils in secondary schools.[9] This in turn may reflect a subtle shift in thinking from debates around whether the parents or teachers are the legitimate source of information towards a more pragmatic concern that children receive adequate information from either parent or school. The key frame of reference, then, is not the home or school but the notion of the informed child, with 'responsible' adult agencies providing the necessary information.

Ironically, the success of a more comprehensive sex education policy could lead to the denial of the kinds of autonomy and rights that adults take for granted as part of their private lives. The partial 'nationalization' of sex education and the pragmatic needs of the wider society may generate more compelling images of the informed child. But in the process sex education exposes children to more and more information within a public arena and potentially denies them the ability to select and control, in effect to manage the information they need to allow them a degree of privacy. Teachers and pupils prefer the informal small group approach to sex education classes. Yet the idea that sex education is part of the pastoral network in schools owes more to its peripheral status *vis-à-vis* the curriculum rather than any notion that sex education has a different pedagogic rationale. One of the problems that teachers have with sex education is the focus on classroom-based instruction (Wyness, 1996). Much of this has to do with their difficulties in working with curricular material that places them in the moral firing line. Teaching sex education makes it more difficult to differentiate the general from the personal or the private. Sex education threatens the teachers' need for professional 'perfectibility' (Hargreaves, 1994) because it generates classroom

weaknesses through levels of embarrassment. An expanding sex education curriculum might have similar effects on pupils. At one level it
'empowers' children by providing them with the information required to
be able to maintain a degree of physical integrity and in some cases
make informed choices. It also incidentally puts children in a stronger
position to embarrass the teacher. At another level there is the opening
up of what little the child has of a private life. An unintentional consequence of sex education on the national curriculum might be the more
comprehensive and overt exposure of the child's sexual and moral
thoughts and feelings.

The loading up of a centrally imposed curriculum and the influence of
a more didactic teaching ideology (see chapter 4) suggest that schools'
resources and energies are directed away from the tutorial room and
'confessional' towards the more traditional sites of learning such as the
whole class (see Gatton, 1998). We might be forgiven for thinking that
the repositioning of teachers as sovereign authority figures at the front of
the classroom prescribing a standard curriculum would further 'publi-
cize' the pupils' ability to manage the sex education curriculum. In
effect, there may be fewer teaching situations that would allow them to
shift between what Goffman termed 'front' and 'back' regions in managing their personal affairs (1959).

We are left here with the feeling that, although there is an urgency
about its implementation, a clumsy, nationally imposed sex education
curriculum will not be able to deal with the subtle nuances of children's
developing sexual understandings and choices. The adult equivalents –
the therapist's couch, the private confessional and the counsellor's circle –
guarantee adults a degree of privacy when sexual matters need to be
dealt with in more professional terms. We come back to the deterministic nature of schooling discussed in chapter 4. The nature of the
curriculum, its content and delivery, the age grading which temporally
positions pupils and the rules and regulations which govern the child's
use of time and space in school, are all factors which structure the child's
school experiences. At the same time there are cultural trends that free up
information and knowledge outside the institution of schooling, namely,
a burgeoning public discourse on sex that cannot be easily contained
within morally acceptable boundaries. The school is trying to regulate
this information – contain it within the segregated and 'exclusive' confines of the classroom. In the process this generates interesting and
potentially conflicting consequences for pupils. Children are partially
incorporated within the adult world of sex and morality, but this is a
heavily regulated process. Nevertheless, the child's 'need to know' now
rivals other political, moral and generational considerations which

surround the sex education debate. At the same time that children are
incorporated within the 'adult world of secrets', the structure of schooling serves to remind them of their subordinate status in the way in
which the knowledge they are now arguably entitled to is conveyed to
them. The attenuation of private spaces for children – the lack of privacy
in school – grows as 'child work' has intensified because of recent education reform. This affects teachers' abilities to prepare, develop and explore
the various facets of their work and importantly restricts the potential
discursive contexts for discussing sexual morality with pupils. Children
are deprived of any sense of privacy because of their lack of ontological
status and because of their very limited ability to influence events in
school have even fewer opportunities for personal and private reflection.

Citizenship Education: the Political Child

Sex education challenges the ideology of innocence whilst making it
more difficult for children to retain any notion of personal privacy. If we
turn to the inclusion of citizenship education within the curriculum, we
might think that schools are being encouraged to turn their attention to
pupils' existing and future commitments within the public realm.
Citizenship education has arguably entered the educational agendas in
various countries because of serious social and public order problems.[10]
In one sense the problems of racism, delinquency and child abuse have
reached such proportions that what was seen as implicit, hidden from, or
peripheral to, the curriculum values are now having to be considered as
prominent features of the pupils' school experience. Citizenship education thus becomes a catch-all which implies a more inclusive attempt at
regulating the child's attitudes and behaviour. What tends to pass as citizenship or moral education in Britain is fragmented, localized and
unsystematic. The centralizing impulses of policy makers are sharpened
in trying to incorporate citizenship and morality within the national curriculum. There is an obvious attraction to a national values or citizenship
curriculum, particularly where prominent educationalists such as the
head of the School Curriculum and Assessment Authority (SCAA) want
to counter an 'all pervasive moral relativism' in British society (*The
Times*, 16 January 1998, p. 2).

   A British government advisory group led by the eminent political sci-
entist Bernard Crick has the responsibility for overseeing the
introduction of citizenship into the national curriculum. In its early
days the advisory group did seem to be under pressure to set down a
more prescriptive moral agenda and one of the key features of the
subsequent report (DfEE, 1998) promotes the strengthening of the

pupil's social and moral responsibility as a key objective of citizenship. But the broad thrust of the report, *Education for Citizenship and the Teaching of Democracy in Schools*, is for the introduction of citizenship education which stresses 'remoralization' as the strengthening of collective commitments and the active involvement of young people in the broader political and civic culture. The authors eschew the problem-driven rationale for citizenship education. They quote approvingly from the British Youth Council's written submission to the advisory group.

> [W]e believe that it is important to set out areas that the [citizenship] curriculum should not cover, or at least be dominated or distracted by. It would be tempting to allow citizenship education to become simply issues based on moral education, revolving around key concepts such as drugs, health education, housing and homelessness . . . We believe that the most important issues facing young people as citizens is their lack of knowledge about society, its democratic process and their actual rights and responsibilities as citizens.
>
> (1998, p. 20)

Thus the report is wary of the influence of single-issue lobbying groups and the potential for citizenship education to be hijacked by particular moral agendas. The only significant problem discussed within the report that the authors feel citizenship education should direct its energies towards is young people's ignorance of and disaffection from the existing political system. I will contend that the report is a competence-based document with an emphasis on community involvement, political participation underpinned by the notion of 'political literacy'. In what follows I examine the document with reference to three areas that challenge the incompetence thesis. First of all, the report states that 'political literacy' levels are low in school because pupils appear to have little understanding of how the political system works. Thus part of the 5 per cent of the national curriculum given over to citizenship education would concentrate on producing a more politically aware school population. From key stage 1 through to key stage 4 the curriculum would consist of knowledge of political institutions, principles and philosophies. Students would also be encouraged to develop discursive skills that would improve their levels of 'political literacy'. There is a developmental frame here in that younger children at key stage 1 would be expected to acquire discursive skills and take progressively more knowledge-based classes as they got older. But the report expects that all classes at all levels would include information and discussion about political cultures around 'controversial issues' relating to political ideology and religious and cultural difference. As with a more inclusive sex education curriculum, there is then a much stronger emphasis on the child's need to know which challenges the ideology of innocence. The report states that it is no longer appropriate to 'shelter our nation's children from even the harsher controversies of adult life, but [the curriculum] should prepare them to deal with such controversies knowledgeably, sensibly, tolerantly and morally' (p. 56).

As well as encouraging pupils to think of how political systems are made up, there is a suggestion that citizenship education would invigorate a present and future civic sphere. A second point relates to the way citizenship education establishes a social and political ontology for children. As I argued in the previous chapter, the educational project parallels the socialization process in that educationalists tend to assume pupils are adults- or citizens-in-waiting. This seems to be a fundamental reason for the exclusion of children from any significant involvement in education matters. T. H. Marshall's classic definition of citizenship is of 'a status bestowed on those who are full members of a community. All who possess the status are equal with respect to rights and duties with which that status is endowed' (1950, pp. 28–29). Marshall goes on to argue that citizenship incorporates a series of rights: civil rights, freedom of thought and speech and a right to own property; political rights which centre on full political participation; and social rights which give access to resources that underpin the individual's physical, educational and social welfare. Clearly children have very few of these rights and thus the idea of children as full citizens in Marshall's terms is somewhat restricted. The *Education for Citizenship* report (DfEE, 1998) envisages citizenship education as a preparation for the child's future role as an informed and committed citizen. At the same time there are grounds for thinking that the report is encouraging children's political participation and a more central role within the public realm. It encourages pupils to become involved in voluntary work and community matters. Political literacy, then, gives children the resources to take a more active interest in and make some sort of contribution to the existing 'public good'. The report is replete with models of 'good practice' which focus on the civic possibilities for pupils. To illustrate: one of the schools mentioned in the report has set up formal links between the school council and the local town council. The Young People's Town Council is made up of pupils from the local secondary school who meet monthly in the town hall and represent the views of local young people. Through this forum young people have been able to place environmental issues and school safety problems on the local political agenda. The report refers to this as the 'empowerment' of children. I have discussed the limitations of this concept in chapter 3. Nevertheless, the point I want to make here is that citizenship education is not simply a preparation for adulthood but deals with the child's here-and-now status as an 'active citizen'. Empowerment at a very basic level here means taking notice of children as existing as well as future citizens.

A shift in the child's ontology is recognized through the child's expected political involvement within the community. A third point relates to the way the child's position within the society is enhanced, as it were, much closer to home through more active participation within the school and classroom. The report hints at a quite different approach to education than was envisaged through the education reforms of the 1980s. There is a rejection of the idea of schooling as a 'scheme of training'. The idea of the child as a relatively passive recipient of a standardized curriculum is eschewed in favour of pupils demonstrating their civic commitment in a discursive and formative role during classroom lessons. There is to be more 'active participation in group decision-making and the development of further qualities of the mind beyond retentive memory' (p. 57). There is also to be a more discursive and influential role for pupils at the school level. The report not surprisingly mentions the 'family resemblance' between citizenship education and whole school approaches. Both are taken to be in a position to force schools to re-evaluate their ethos and underlying values with respect to the active citizenry of pupils in school. Specific mention is made of pupils' organizational and 'political' involvement in school. The report, for example, highlights the democratic possibilities of pupil councils and explores the possibility that they become compulsory elements of a school infrastructure (p. 25). Thus political literacy is not extended simply through a knowledge base but put into political practice. In other words, a curriculum on democracy should be reflected in a more democratic pedagogy.

Advocacy

Although the report takes a quite refreshing child-oriented approach to the business of children's political knowledge and participation, there is an absence of any consideration of the role that a child advocate might play. Now this may have been outside the specific remit of the advisory group – the emphasis is much more on curricular issues. Nevertheless, the notion of empowerment, the promotion of a more politically active youth and the whole notion of political literacy are suggestive of children having a more formal political voice. Given also that this issue was discussed by the Labour Party in the late 1980s, it is surprising that serious consideration has not been given to child advocacy at school, LEA or national levels (Labour Party, 1989).

The precedent for an advocate of sorts has been set in this country within the child-care context (see chapter 2). The 1989 Children Act in Britain extends the role of the guardian *ad litem* in mediating between children and the institutional adult world. Young children's voices and opinions are heard through an adult whose role is to convey the child's interests to an adult audience of social workers and court officials. We can also refer to initiatives set up independently of the legislation. Several local authorities have introduced Children's Rights Officers whose remit is to deal with complaints children have whilst in local authority care and offer support for them. Whilst these officers have limited powers and their work is restricted to a minority of children, those within the child-care system, they do have some local clout, as Franklin and Franklin (1996) illustrate in their review of the children's rights movement. Finally, there is a range of children's organizations that now provide an *ad hoc* advocacy service such as Voice for the Child in Child Care, and the Children Society (Lyon, 1997).

Two factors might give us grounds for thinking that an institutional structure which strengthens the child's voice within a child-care context ought to follow within an educational context. First, the principle of the Children Act is the paramountcy of the child's welfare. If we accept that the child's welfare incorporates the education of the child, then this has clear implications for the treatment of children within schools. Second, child-care policy overlaps with education in respect to child protection. I discussed in chapter 3 the importance of the school as a forum for child abuse prevention strategies. Schools have also become more formative in detecting abuse. For instance, the circular 10/95 'Protecting Children from Abuse' was sent to all primary and secondary schools in England and Wales in 1996. The information in the circular recognizes that schools are crucial sites for the identification of abuse and generates expectations that all schools will have specially designated teachers trained to deal with the various implications of child abuse.

Despite these trends, Britain lags behind other countries in Europe, North America and Australasia, where child advocates are established at various political levels of representation. Two examples will suffice. In New Zealand a child advocate has been appointed at the local urban level in Christchurch as a way of improving the lines of communication and modes of participation between children and local government (Christchurch City Council, 1997). In this situation the establishing of a political voice for children is part of a broader strategy to increase community involvement in urban matters. Children here are thus much more fully integrated into the political mainstream as citizens. Now, although nothing explicit is stated about pupil participation in Christchurch schools, education as well as health, welfare security and recreation are all part of this urban shift towards local participation. The documentation refers to 'networks', 'focus groups' and 'brainstorming', some of which we might expect to take place in schools.

In the Norwegian case the child advocate as an ombudsman occupies a powerful role at the national political centre, with direct access to government and the media. Malfrid Flekkoy (1988, p. 308), the first incumbent of this position, sets out the rationale for the ombudsman as an 'independent spokesman, national defender and public conscience arouser on behalf [of children]'. Interestingly, Flekkoy contends that children need to be treated differently from adults by the criminal justice system and in terms of protecting their rights to welfare. Yet it would be a mistake to see this as using the position of ombudsman to marginalize in some formal sense the position of children. Whilst Flekkoy argues that children's needs are different from those of adults, these needs are, nevertheless, to be articulated politically in terms of rights. These rights are to be both protected and represented at the highest political levels, which in some respects brings children on a par with adults with respect to claims that can be made on the state. For instance, the ombudsman is well placed to counter the complete disregard of children's rights in school. The author lists school exclusion or sacking and health and safety matters as illustrations of areas where teachers have some say through their conditions of employment. Children, other than making informal representations to their parents, have no control over their working conditions in school.

Conclusion

There are few common empirical and historical threads here linking the introduction of peer mediation in English primary schools to a 'nationalized' sex education curriculum and the recent publication promoting the teaching of citizenship. We can refer to the historically weak tradition of both educating children in sexual and political matters and encouraging pupil participation in school affairs in Britain. We can also point to the comparative underdevelopment of these educational areas in Britain in global terms. What we have is a range of policy initiatives that exist at the interstices of education reform. They first of all act as localized challenges to national trends. Peer mediation, for instance, in the central England region, is an important element of local education policy largely initiated at grassroots level with the support of the region's chief executive, a relentless critic of the reforms discussed in chapter 4. The broad thrust of policy at this local level is to 'remoralize' teachers as well as empower pupils and encourage greater pupil involvement. Peer mediation was seen as a way of countering an over-centralised and bureaucratized curriculum which alienated and demoralized both teachers and pupils. It is also worth mentioning that this region has urban centres densely populated by children from ethnic minorities. Although there are no figures for this region, anecdotal evidence suggests that peer mediation has been taken up by many primary schools with high proportions of children with Asian backgrounds. These schools are pursuing a whole range of high-profile anti-racism strategies. Now, although these strategies are a result of decades of inner-city problems that have afflicted children from ethnic minorities (see chapter 4) there are some grounds for thinking that education reform, particularly the national curriculum, was addressing children's entitlements from within the cultural mainstream. Education reform is potentially alienating children from ethnic minority groups. Peer mediation may therefore be an important means of strengthening the personal and collective position of those children on the cultural margins.

A second characteristic of these initiatives is that they have developed from areas that have been marginalized in the curriculum. Partly because they cannot be satisfactorily assessed, partly because of their weak historical backgrounds, sex, politics and health have traditionally come under the umbrella area of Personal and Social Education (PSE), which has usually been dealt with in an *ad hoc* and unsystematic manner by the political centre. As concerns over values, public order and protection have become progressively more central, so these issues have crept on to the national educational agenda. The values shift towards responsibility, accountability and blame (discussed in chapter 2) identifies schools as responsible agents for moral and civic failures regardless of their origins. At the same time, schools connect with broader counter-cultural pressures such as the expansion of information and knowledge and the nascent and amorphous demands for greater children's rights. Sex and citizenship education can be seen as attempts by schools to mediate these conflicting pressures.

Where these initiatives converge is on the idea of the child as citizen. First, there is an emphasis on children's rights to knowledge which strengthens their ability to make informed choices on a range of issues relating to their own personal, physical and moral integrity. Sex education and citizenship education, along with child abuse prevention programmes, assume that children are confident enough to handle a range of such information. Second, there is an emphasis on children participating in areas that are largely the province of adults in authority. Peer mediation structures young children's formative roles in the playground and classroom by encouraging them to take responsibility for supervision and to keep the peace. Citizenship education provides a broader political context for these initiatives: there is both an expansion of knowledge and the provision of a framework that encourages pupil involvement in decision-making processes. This is potentially an important shift in thinking about childhood. In chapter 4 education reform produced a more intensive and carefully regulated *schooled* version of childhood (Hendrick, 1997). Educational, psychological and sociological theory tends to justify the way in which schools act on children as a preparation for future moral, social, political and economic positions in society. In effect, children here are citizens-in-waiting. The initiatives discussed in this chapter draw the concept of childhood within the debates around the social and political significance of citizenship. There is some scope, then, for at least rethinking the ontological status of children as citizens rather than trainees.

Whether this rethink leads to a renegotiation of the status boundary between pupil and teacher, child and adult, depends largely on a series of adult imperatives: control, protection and socialization. In her analysis of peer support networks, Sharp (1996) contends that a child's right to confidentiality when working through problems in school with other pupils will always be compromised by the teacher's responsibility to protect and advise. Children's school lives are always ultimately regulated by adult interests (see chapter 4). The adult–child boundary nevertheless does not always have to be conceptualized in zero-sum terms. A strengthening of adult regulation does not always lead to a correlative reduction in a child's autonomy. I cannot go along with Postman's (1983) notion that knowledge is something that is monopolized by adults as a way of maintaining their authority. Knowledge is ultimately something that is more likely to be shared across borders and boundaries (Giddens, 1984). As was discussed in the Crick Report, there is no reason to think that improving children's access to knowledge on moral, sexual and political issues will undermine the authority of adults.

Conclusion

Institutional Contexts

One of the key themes running through education reform has been the localization of ownership of and responsibility for education. Parents have been recentred as consumers, guardians and guarantors of their children's schooling. One of the themes running through this book is that public perception, social policy prescription and social scientific research still tend to target the family and the parent as the responsible agent. The underlying notions of nature, of biology and of social need endorse the power of family, usually at the expense of other institutions that have claims on the child's welfare. The family is quintessentially the unit that embodies and produces individuals and an ethic of individualism. Within a relatively isolated and emotionally self-sufficient unit, children are controlled and protected by individually responsible parents who promote and support the development of the rational individual. From the outside children are subject to the imperatives of development and socialization – a period of dependence in all respects on their parents – a necessary precondition of their futures as individuals. They are accounted for by parents and in general their provisional social status absorbs them within the structures of family.

In this book I refer to a culture of blame which creates conflicting pressures for parents. Parents are targeted as responsible agents in that they are brought to account for the perceived moral and educational failings of their children. Delinquency, truancy and school aggression are traced back to what parents do or fail to do to their children, normally in the early years. A culture of blame also denotes a pathology of social problems which takes an extreme form of individualism, particularly where these problems centre around children's moral and physical welfare. Whilst parents might be blamed for what their children do within the public arena, where violence and abuse are perpetrated on children, where children are defined as victims, such 'acts' are framed in terms of particular types of abusers: abusing families and abusing classes. I argued in chapter 3 that this normalizes, and magnifies the importance of the institution of family and the structures of adult and parental authority. It thus conceals possible structural features of the problem that alert us to the possibility that the very normality of family, parental authority and adult protection provides opportunities for the sexual abuse of children. We might therefore speculate that the home is an environment offering few possibilities for the child as a social agent. Despite the convergence of pressures on parents, we might be suggesting that compared to institutions like the school, parents have a much stronger sense of ownership of the child.

Whilst the very structure of family will always compromise the view that children are members of a minority social group, the new childhood studies have tackled the structural position of children by identifying the possibilities for childhood agency within the home. The work of Berry Mayall (1996) is illuminating here. Her research with mothers and their small children highlights the negotiable and practical character of parent–child relations. It does not challenge family boundaries for the simple reason that, in a phenomenological sense, children help to create boundaries and relations within family. Family here is viewed as a microsociety, what Mayall calls a 'social order', where there is a much more dynamic form of socialization and more attention is given to the formative roles that children play. If we compare this with the other dominant site for children, the school, there is sense in which rules are being framed and reframed by children. Processes of individualization take the classic liberal form in schools in that they limit social membership to those who are considered rational and responsible. Although family personifies this individualism through its social position and responsibilities in the way in which children are subsumed, the school, particularly the post-reform school, denies children any informal access to the structures and resources within school or, more broadly, within the education market-place which would help make a difference. Children are both ontologically absent and perceived as being socially incompetent – unfit to reflect on school choice and policy.

Yet, as with family, there are pressures and counter-pressures that both tighten and loosen the grip that schools have on children. There are two sets of forces worth mentioning which threaten even the most powerful educational minds and impel practitioners to take up more defensive positions of control. First, the political agenda of 'improving standards' and 'school efficiency' creates a more bureaucratic and intensive atmosphere within schools where pupils are acted on as educational objects and processed through a series of stages with reference to mea-surable outcomes. As I argued in chapter 2, pupils become important units in making teachers more accountable. Second, the culture of blame which targets parents hovers over schools and extends educational net-works of accountability into a broader social arena. Delinquency and truancy are framed in terms of children being 'out of place', forcing educationalists to develop a range of ties with the broader community. As the educational frame of reference is widened in the pursuit of solu-tions to the problem of educational disorder, the culture of blame also creates more defensive practices as teachers have to account for their performances, generate a positive market image of the school to prospec-tive consumers and square this with the negative images of teaching portrayed by the media. This defensiveness means that teachers are more likely to err on the side of parsimony with respect to incorporating the views and opinions of pupils.

Whilst recent education reform has not created a more inclusive work-ing environment for teachers and pupils, there are counter-pressures. I briefly refer to the contentious issue of child-centredness in chapter 4. I drew on Pollard's (1996) observation that teachers try and hold on to more informal child-centred approaches as a means of protecting chil-dren from the pressures of an overloaded curriculum. Whilst the notion of protection is hardly a recipe for more pupil involvement, Pollard (1996) goes along with Sugrue (1997) in his notion that child-centred-ness is a question of value and commitment rather than the simple practical expression of a professed ideology. Sugrue takes various educa-tional thinkers to task for categorizing teachers as either 'child-centred' or 'traditionalists'. According to Sugrue, teachers use a mixture of approaches depending on context and purpose. The observable prac-tices, the much maligned notion of spontaneity and free play, if drawn on at all are a means to the end of pushing children's learning to the limits. Sugrue, then, sees good teaching as a matter of commitment to and engagement with pupils. Whilst his research does no more than illus-trate what has probably always been the case in primary schools, and there is little sense in which children are being liberated or empowered, he highlights a set of teaching values and commitments that generate teaching practices that work 'with' rather than 'on' children.

A second set of counter-pressures are of a rather different order. They relate to a contrast between the position of children within the school and rapid changes to their working environment. Children's lack of influence, the absence of any channels that would make the curriculum, school management or the teaching staff in any way accountable, is starkly offset by rapid technological change which draws children into a complex global system of information and a more anarchic series of relations between users of technology. There is a very strange juxtaposition here: a technologically sophisticated and highly individualized information network and a rather antiquated set of social relationships between pupils and staff. There are two ways of viewing this. We can refer back to Postman (1982) and the 'crisis of childhood' thesis. Here the rise of the Internet challenges the boundaries between adults and children. The old certainties of childhood are represented in the school system, which is having to cope with newer, more disruptive sources of knowledge not only easily accessible to children but monopolized by children relative to adults. A second interpretation would see the Internet as a simple illustration of the way in which structural shifts in society incorporate children as competent social actors. In chapter 5, I examined a possible resolution of this tension through the way in which policy at national and local level is tapping into more global trends and addressing children as people who have a right to be informed.

Policy Dimension

Childhood has become a key theme within the policy realm. Not only does this contribute to a heightened awareness of childhood as a social problem, but it focuses private and public attention on whatever institutional means are available to sustain the idea of childhood. Whilst epistemologies and professional practices are quite different, the exigencies of child protection and welfare are now such that professional and academic boundaries between education, social care and the criminal justice system are less important than the broad range of problems confronting professionals, families and children. In the previous section I suggested that the relations between adults and children at home can be viewed differently from those at school. If we draw on the corresponding policy domains for each institution, they converge at certain points.

Child protection is an overarching theme here. Traditionally the preserve of the social services and the criminal justice system, schools have become more involved in identifying 'children at risk'. Schools are also the sites of a range of different preventive approaches which draw on quite different assumptions about young children. Despite the reticence of some of these programmes to examine the 'normality' of child sexual abuse, young children are being encouraged to confront quite difficult, possibly disturbing images and material. A third 'child-care theme' to work its way through the education system is the issue of aggression and bullying. As with CAPP, these problems are tackled when children are still relatively young. As with CAPP, peer mediation tackles the problem by equipping children with the necessary resources – the concept of empowerment, despite its limitations, comes to mind here as a common approach to dealing with threats to children's physical integrity. Finally, again as with CAPP, peer mediation potentially threatens the unconditional nature of adult responsibility and authority. CAPP generate more questioning of a parent's taken-for-granted rights to the child's physical integrity – it creates a new set of 'children's rights' – a right to their own physical boundaries. Peer mediation, although carefully regulated by teachers, still disrupts the normal distribution of school responsibilities among teaching staff – discipline and policing matters are now distributed among the pupil population, for some teachers the crossing of an educational Rubicon.

In chapter 3 I addressed the contested position of children within the criminal justice system. First, children, particularly those who have been traumatized by sexual abuse, need to be protected from the harsh realities of the police interview room and the courtroom. These are children who fail the system because the system has failed them. These are children unable to participate. Second, there is the more recent image of the child as a reliable witness. Backed up by an array of psychological research and driven by the political and professional need for justice, children are now potentially more active and formative within the system. Finally, there is a third group of children who are responsible legal subjects. Legal responsibility might be read from the qualifications of the reliable witness; competence does presuppose a degree of individualism. Like child abuse, this offers a darker, negative side of childhood; yet there is a significant shift from victim to protagonist or offender. Thus, unlike the young abused child who can be easily accommodated within existing conceptual schemes, the very young child as offender does not readily fit with the conventional view of childhood, nor for that matter does he or she correspond to the adult version of criminal liability or responsibility (Jenks, 1996).

Global Context

An important feature of the global picture of childhood is the alleged exportation of 'childhood' (Boyden, 1997; Stephens, 1995). We have here a global version of the 'childhood in crisis' thesis. Childhood assumes a single form, presented as a universal model and expressed in terms of the need to bring the 'world's children' up to a basic standard. From a cultural or social constructionist perspective the 'world's children' is read as an emotive cover for a western and welfarist conception of childhood which only applies within specific historical and cultural conditions. Stephens views the United Nations Convention on the Rights of the Child in precisely these terms. Her suspicions are grounded in the idea that global capitalism is the cultural and economic frame of reference for the Convention. More specifically, an emphasis on rights and contract and the 'individual' child hints at a welfarist conception of childhood. As she sets out: 'its [UN's] declaration of universal children's rights gives children the right to be remade in the image of adults and non-Western childhoods the right to be remade in Western forms' (1995, p. 36). Whilst we might question the first part of the quote – the extent to which children have been granted rights to self-determination – I want to draw attention to the second problem, of exporting a welfarist version of childhood. There are two assumptions here: that there is a single unambiguous model of the welfare child and that welfare is a compelling global frame of reference. First of all, I would hope to have dispelled the notion in this book that from within a western and welfarist context there is an unambiguous model of childhood. If I can refer back to my discussion of rights in the introductory chapter: a welfarist model, because it assumes protection rather than participation, contradicts any notion that children might have the same rights as adults. The 'rights' model, in its self-determinist form, which is explicit in the first part of the Stephens' quote, is far too imprecise a model. Whilst children might be more involved in criminal and legal processes, in chapter 3 I set out the different ways that children are treated within the criminal justice system. If by welfarist Stephens is referring to the protected and schooled versions, then again, in this book I have set out a more contested version of childhood in the policy domain. As regards the second assumption, if a welfarist version is being exported as an implicit model of 'good practice', then it is taking place at a point in time where western welfare states are being attacked and restructured. The exporting of the welfare child into developing countries is taking place at a time when welfare is under attack in these countries. To take the example of Britain: I have drawn out the influence of the market within education and the increasing elaboration of systems of accountability in the broader policy domain which at the very least compromise the social democratic underpinnings of welfare that had been its mainstay from the post-war period until the 1970s.

Childhood and Individualization

My final comments refer back to the discussion of theories of late modernity in chapter 1. Individualization, social fragmentation and social reconfiguration are now familiar refrains within sociological theory.

Individuals are freer now in their ability to shift between a range of cultural reference points. What this implies is that dimensions such as social class, gender and social geography are less compelling frames of reference. The debate within sociological theory between the modernist notion of 'dominant' mediating institutions and the idea of the 'biographical project' has ignored the possibilities for viewing childhood as a variable of social analysis. Generational frames are nowhere to be seen: children are either invisible or sanctified as the last repository of a disappearing modernist order. Childhood, if you like, exposes the limits of individualization theory whilst providing the perennial but hidden basis of individualism. The new sociology of childhood, especially work carried out at the European level, takes a more positive view in recognizing the status of the child as a member of a minority group. It will be interesting to see whether childhood or generation compete with 'older' stratifying systems such as gender and social class or whether a generational frame of reference is viewed more as a feature of a socially fragmented and individualized reference point for social identity formation. Either way, I have argued in this book that childhood should assume the status of a contested but ontologically established framework for analysis. This largely reflects the view that adults working with children are being forced to take more notice of what children do and who they are in public as well as private matters. This in turn generates different and sometimes unexpected relations between adults and children. In short, these relations encourage us to think about the institution of childhood in more contested terms.

Appendix
A Comment on the Data

In chapter 5 I have drawn on material from a small-scale project which assesses the introduction and reception of peer mediation in schools within a large city in the centre of England. There is no attempt to generalize from a largely unrepresentative sample of pupils and teachers. The material is used for illustrative and suggestive purposes only. The project was carried out in 1995 and was made up of three elements.

- 108 peer mediators aged between 6 and 17 who attended a conference organized by peer mediators themselves were surveyed on a range of issues relating to their roles as mediators.
- A semi-structured focus group interview with seven peer mediators who attended the conference was conducted with the express purpose of tapping into their broader perceptions of peer mediation.
- Questionnaires were sent to 32 head teachers who had recently introduced some form of peer mediation into their schools. The aim here was to gather some basic information and gauge the opinion of teachers on peer mediation as they saw it in their schools. Information on the relevant schools was obtained from peer mediation consultants who had been working with schools for several years.

Notes

Introduction

1 Yet see Corsaro's (1997, pp. 54–65) interesting account of how children's social influence in historical terms has been obscured from view and how a 'new history of childhood' reveals the formative role of children in specific historical settings.

1 Childhood in Crisis

1 In a later book Harris (1983) refers to the gendered nature of this dependency. Women, because of their imputed child-rearing responsibilities, are more likely to experience a sense of powerlessness as parents than their male counterparts.

2 See, for example, Jones and Wallace (1990) and several of the other articles in Bates and Riseborough (eds) (1993). Whilst accepting the cultural importance of individualization, these writers emphasize a structural material realm in which choice and opportunity are still distributed according social class and gender.

3 A survey conducted by Kidscape in 1994 of 1,000 parents found that 97 per cent of parents mentioned possible child abduction as their biggest fear about their children (*The Times*, 10 February 1994).

4 See Nasman's limited legal application of the term (1994, pp. 167–168).

2 Social Policy and Moral Ambiguity

1 Home is in quotes here because where children are not living in conventional families – households with at least one parent present – in most cases there is an attempt to create a 'family' environment where biological family is missing.

2 Arguably we are talking about mothers here.

3 There is an interesting tension in the usage of nature here. Parental authority is natural and therefore to be freed whilst children are to be more closely

controlled because of their proximity to nature. See Gittins (1998, pp. 38–42) for an extended discussion of the inconsistent usage of nature.

4 See Eekelaar (1991) for more detail on the first two conceptions.

5 There seem to be elements of both 'obligations' and 'blame' in Etzioni's theory of communitarianism. The traditional refrain 'too many rights, too few responsibilities' forms the basis of his book, *The Spirit of the Community* (1993).

6 For example, see Waslander and Thrupp (1996) on New Zealand, and Chubb and Moe (1990) on the United States.

7 It must be noted that the current Labour government is intending to abolish selection on 'parental' criteria. See the White Paper, *Excellence in Schools* (1997, p. 71).

8 See Carroll and Walford (1996) and Ball, Bowe and Gerwitz (1995) for discussions of a localized education market.

9 Whilst social workers are not subject to the disciplines of the market in quite such an explicit way as teachers, a recent policy document on quality protection programmes (Department of Health, 1998) couches localized accountability in terms of 'Management Action Plans' and 'national government objectives' for children's services, the former being inspected in terms of the latter.

10 Interestingly, the rights movement here is reminiscent of calls for parent power in education with rights as powers overshadowing a rather underdeveloped sense of obligations.

3 Child Sexual Abuse

1 In Britain there has been a series of abuse cases involving local authority institutions.

2 There has been a series of recent cases of parents and stepparents being taken to court in Britain by their children for using corporal punishment. One case has set a legal precedent of sorts in that a 9-year-old boy successfully took his stepfather to the European Court of Human Rights for beating him with a garden cane. The Labour government accepts the Court's decision that the father's treatment was 'abusive', but still wants to retain parents' rights to smack their children. See *The Times*, 24 September 1998, p. 1.

3 For example, the seminal *Constructing and Reconstructing Childhood* by James and Prout, first published in 1990, had little or no discussion of biological differences. Compare this with James, Jenks and Prout's later (1998) *Theorising Childhood*, where there is a chapter devoted to biology: 'The body and childhood'.

4 The book does refer to a cousin being abused by his father.

5 A theme to be taken up in chapter 4.

6 For example, Parents Against Injustice (PAIN). See La Fontaine (1990).

7 Cross et al.'s (1995) main concern is to highlight the fact that dramatic events like court cases involving child witnesses are rare. Although 54 per cent of cases are carried forward to trial, only 9 per cent of cases involve

children giving evidence in court as the great majority of 'successful' cases result in the offender pleading guilty. The problem for the child witnesses is not so much the drama of the courtroom as the more mundane and protracted but equally stressful run-up to a prospective trial.

8   It is worth pointing to the different usages of LTL in Scotland and England and Wales. In the former context LTL covers all cases concerning children; in the latter context LTL is used only in cases of abuse.

9   See the report in *The Guardian,* 'Satanic Verses', 10 September 1994.

4 Childhood, Agency and Education Reform

1   See chapter 1 on Alanen (1998) and her 'top-down' and 'bottom-up' approach.

2   There are implications to be drawn from ethnographic work on children's minority status in school. But the influence of class, gender and ethnicity are usually taken as more formative.

3   Harris (1991) argues that the emphasis on children's participation here reflects the promotion of sound classroom management rather than any moral notion of children's right to be heard. Given that this recommendation is so out of step with education reform itself, there are good grounds for being cynical about the underlying rationale for pupil participation. Yet we cannot completely dismiss this recommendation. Taking a more democratic approach to the problem of discipline in schools, whether it be for pragmatic or moral reasons, gives pupils some say in school affairs.

4   This is not to say that pupils are not aware of the implications of testing. In a recent small-scale project assessing education reform from primary pupils' perspectives, I report on the connections that pupils made between testing and the public perceptions of both teachers and schools. See Wyness and Silcock, forthcoming.

5   The statementing of special educational needs pupils involves a formal assessment of the pupil. On the basis of the assessment, funds are released for supporting the pupil.

6   The report does acknowledge that some progress was made in the schools that were revisited.

5 Childhood and Citizenship

1   For more detail on the research see the appendix.

2   Two factors might account for these sectoral differences: peer mediation was not as well established in secondary as primary schools as it had only recently been introduced in the former; second, status and peer esteem might be more significant in secondary than primary schools. Older children may be more conscious of the importance of peer relations than younger children.

3   See, for example, Cooper, 1971; Holt, 1975.

4 Clause 28 was effectively rescinded by the 1986 Education Bill which gave school governing bodies responsibility for sex education. This in turn has been superseded by the 1993 Education Act.

5 The recent lowering of the age of consent to 18 for homosexuality suggests some sort of compromise.

6 Lees (1993) contends that AIDS and HIV information circulated freely and sex education which has focused on these topics has not changed the sexual practices of young people.

7 As well as information on sex, the health education lobby is concerned to make children more aware of the dangers of smoking and the use of illegal substances. More recently the latter has been controversially highlighted in the media as drug awareness education is introduced into some primary schools in England and Wales.

8 Within the context of a quasi-market a school's sex education policy becomes part of the paraphernalia of choice as sex education becomes a more visible if not more important feature of the school's infrastructure. It is too early to say whether this may in fact increase the entitlement rights of children to sex education. As was argued in chapter 2, research on the education market indicates a very limited conception of the consumer, with parents rather than children targeted.

9 As far as the absence of sex education within primary schools goes, see Morris, Reid and Fowler (1993).

10 See Viola (1997) and Sears and Hughes (1996) for discussions of the situations in Australia and Canada respectively.

References

Adalbjarnardottir, S. (1994) 'Understanding children and ourselves: teachers' reflections on social development in the classroom', *Teaching and Teacher Education* 10, 4, pp. 409–421.

Advice Group on Citizenship (1998) *Education for Citizenship and the Teaching of Democracy in Schools*, London: Qualifications and Curriculum Authority.

Aggleton, P. (1988) 'Young people, sexuality education and AIDS', *Youth and Policy*, 23, 2, pp. 79–96.

Alanen, L. (1998) 'Children and the family order: constraints and competencies', in I. Hutchby and J. Moran-Ellis (eds) *Children and Social Competence*, London: Falmer Press, pp. 29–45.

Alexander, R., Rose, J. and Woodhead, C. (1992) *Curriculum Organisation and Classroom Practice in Primary Schools*, London: HMSO.

Archard, D. (1993) *Children: rights and childhood*, London: Routledge.

Aries, P. (1961) *Centuries of Childhood*, Harmondsworth: Penguin.

Armstrong, D. and Galloway, D. (1996) 'Children's perceptions of professionals in SEN', in R. Davie and D. Galloway (eds) *Listening to Children in Education*, London: David Fulton, pp. 109–120.

Arnot, M., David, M. and Weiner, G. (1996) *Educational Reforms and Gender Equality in Schools*, London: Equal Opportunities Commission.

Asquith, S. (1996) 'When children kill children: the search for justice', *Childhood: a global journal of child research*, 3, 1, pp. 99–116.

Ball, S. (1994) *Education Reform*, Buckingham: Open University Press.

Ball, S., Bowe, R. and Gewirtz, S. (1995) 'Circuits of schooling: a sociological exploration of parental choice of school in social class contexts', *Sociological Review*, 43, 1, pp. 52–78.

Barber, M. (1992) 'An entitlement curriculum: a strategy for the nineties', *Journal of Curriculum Studies*, 24, 5, pp. 449–455.

Bates, I. and Riseborough, G. (eds) (1993) *Youth and Inequality*, Buckingham: Open University Press.

Beck, U. (1987) 'Beyond status and class', in W. Mega et al. (eds) *Modern German Sociology*, Columbia: Columbia University Press, pp. 57–82.

Beck, U. (1991) *Risk Society*, London: Sage.

Boyden, J. (1997) 'Childhood and the policy makers: a comparative perspective on the globalisation of childhood', in A. James and A. Prout (eds) *Constructing and Reconstructing Childhood*, 2nd edition, London: Falmer Press, pp. 190–229.

Bray, M. (1991) *Sexual Abuse: the child's view*, London: Jessica Kingsley.

Buchner, P. (1990) 'Growing up in the eighties: changes in the social biography of childhood in FRG', in L. Chisholm et al. (eds) *Childhood, Youth and Social Change*, Basingstoke: Falmer Press, pp. 71–84.

Cahill, S. (1990) 'Childhood and public life: reaffirming biographical divisions', *Social Problems*, 37, 3, pp. 390–402.

Carlen, P., Gleeson, D. and Wardhaugh, J. (1992) *Truancy: the politics of compulsory schooling*, Buckingham: Open University Press.

Carroll, S. and Walford, G. (1996) 'A panic about school choice', *Educational Studies*, 22, 3, pp. 393–407.

Carroll, S. and Walford, G. (1997) *Educational Management and Administration*, 25, 2, pp. 169–180.

Central Statistical Office (1994) *Social Focus on Children*, London: HMSO.

Charter, D. (1995) 'Schools threatened by violence', *The Times*, 28 December, p. 6.

Children's Rights Development Unit (1994) *UK Agenda for United Nations Convention on the Rights of the Child*, London: CRDU.

Christchurch City Council (1997) *Strategy for Children: looking after our children – and our city*, Christchurch: Christchurch City Council.

Chubb, J. and Moe, T. (1990) *Pupils, Markets and America's Schools*, Washington: Brookings Institute.

Cobley, C. (1991) 'Child victims of sexual abuse and the criminal justice system in England and Wales', *Journal of Social Welfare and Family Law*, 3, pp. 362–374.

Cohen J. (1993) 'Hi-tech plan to prevent another Bulger tragedy', *Sunday Times*, 21 November, p. 3.

Cooper, D. (1971) *The Death of the Family*, Harmondsworth: Penguin.

Corsaro, W. (1997) *The Sociology of Childhood*, California: Pine Forge.

Cowie, H., Murray, C. and Brooks, L. (1996) 'How effective are peers in tackling bullying?', paper presented to EERA conference, Seville.

Cowie, H. and Sharp, S. (1996) 'Peer counselling in schools: a time to listen', *British Journal of Educational Psychology*, 21, 2, pp. 557–558.

Croll, P. (1996) 'A curriculum for all? Special education needs and the national curriculum', in P. Croll (ed.) *Teachers, Pupils and Primary Schooling*, London: Cassell, pp. 135–145.

Cross, T., Whitcomb, D. and de Vos, E. (1995) 'Criminal justice outcomes of the prosecution of child sex abuse', *Child Abuse and Neglect*, 19, 12, pp. 1431–1442.

Cullingford, C. (1991) *The Inner World of the School*, London: Cassell.

Davies, L. (1994) 'Can students make a difference? International perspectives on transformative education', *International Studies in the Sociology of Education*, 4, 1, pp. 43–56.

Dennis, N. and Erdos, G. (1992) *Families without Fatherhood*, London: Institute of Economic Affairs.

Department of Education (1988) *Education Reform Act*, London: HMSO.

Department for Education (1994) *Our Children's Education: the updated Parent's Charter*, London: Department for Education.

Department for Education and Employment (1991/1994) *Parent's Charter*, London: HMSO.

Department for Education and Employment (1994) *Code of Practice on Identification and Assessment of Special Educational Needs*, London: HMSO.

Department for Education and Employment (1995) *Protecting Children from Abuse: the role of the Education Service*, circular number 10/95, London: DfEE Publications.

Department for Education and Employment (1997) *Excellence in Schools*, London: HMSO.

Department of Education and Science (1992) *Education (Schools) Act, 1992*, London: HMSO.

Department of Health (1992) *Health of the Nation*, London: HMSO.

Department of Health (1998) *Quality Protects*, http://www. doh.gov.uk/quality.htm.

Dhooper, S. and Schneider, P. (1995) 'Evaluation of a school-based child-abuse prevention programme', *Research on Social Work Practice*, 5, 1, pp. 36–46.

Dingwall R., Eekelaar, J. and Murray, T. (1995) *The Protection of Children: state intervention and family life*, 2nd edition, Oxford: Blackwell.

Donzelot, J. (1977) *The Policing of Families*, London: Hutchinson.

Dunn, J. (1988) *The Beginnings of Social Understanding*, Oxford: Blackwell.

Eekelaar, J. (1991) 'State of nature or nature of the state', *Journal of Social Welfare and Family Law* 1, pp. 37–50.

Elias, N. (1998) 'The civilising of parents', in J. Goudsblom and S. Mennell (eds) *The Norbert Elias Reader*, Oxford: Blackwell, pp. 1–17.

Elliott, M. (1985) *Child Sexual Assault: a practical guide to talking with children*, London: Child Assault Prevention Programme.

Elliott, M. (1989) *Dealing with Child Abuse: the Kidscape training guide*, London: Kidscape.

Elliott, M. (1994) *Willow Street Kids – Be Smart, Be Safe*, London: Kidscape.

Elton Report (1989) *Discipline in Schools*, London: HMSO.

Entwistle, N. (1974) *Child-Centred Education*, London: Methuen.

Epstein, D. (1993) 'Too small to notice? Constructions of childhood and discourse of "race" in predominantly white contexts', *Curriculum Studies*, 1, 3, pp. 317–334.

Etzioni, A. (1993) *The Spirit of the Community: rights, responsibilities and the communitarian agenda*, New York: Crown.

Farson, R. (1978) *Birthrights*, New York: Penguin.

Field, N. (1995) 'The child as labourer and consumer: the disappearance of childhood in contemporary Japan', in S. Stephens (ed.) *Childhood and the Politics of Culture*, Princeton, N.J.: Princeton University Press, pp. 51–78.

Fielding, N. and Conroy, S. (1992) 'Interviewing child victims: police and social work investigations of child sex Abuse', *Sociology*, 26, 1, pp. 103–124.

Finkelhor, D. (1988) *Nursery Crimes*, London: Sage.

Flekkoy, M. (1988) 'Child advocacy in Norway', *Children and Society*, 4, pp. 307–318.

Flyn, R. and Bull, R. (1990) 'Child witnesses in Scottish criminal proceedings', in J. Spencer et al. (eds) *Children's Evidence in Legal Proceedings: an international perspective*, Cambridge: University of Cambridge, pp. 102–120.

Fogelman, K. (1991) 'Citizenship in secondary schools: the national picture', in K. Fogelman (ed.) *Citizenship in Schools*, London: David Fulton, pp. 35–48.

Fox-Harding, L. (1991) *Perspectives in Child Care Policy*, London: Longman.

Franklin, A. and Franklin, B. (1996) 'Growing pains: the developing children's rights movement in the UK', in J. Pilcher and S. Wagg (eds) *Thatcher's Children?* London: Falmer Press, pp. 94–113.

Freeman, M. (1983) *The Rights and Wrongs of Children*, London: Frances Pinter.

Freeman, M. (1992) *Children, their Families and the Law*, Basingstoke: Macmillan.

Galloway, D. (1990) 'Was the GERBIL a Marxist mole?', in P. Evans and V. Varma (eds) *Special Education: past, present and future*, Lewes: Falmer Press, pp. 78–97.

Gatton, M. (1998) 'Back to consulting the ORACLE', *Times Education Supplement*, 3 July, p. 24.

Giddens, A. (1984) *The Constitution of Society*. Cambridge: Polity Press.

Giddens, A. (1990) *The Consequences of Modernity*, Cambridge: Polity Press.

Giddens, A. (1992) *Modernity and Self-Identity: self and society in the modern age*, Cambridge: Polity Press.

Gilder, G. (1982) *Wealth and Poverty*, London: Buchan and Enright.

Gillborn, D. (1996) *Recent Research on the Achievements of Ethnic Minority Pupils*, London: HMSO.

Gittins, D. (1998) *The Child in Question*, Basingstoke: Macmillan.

Goffman, E. (1959) *The Presentation of Self in Everyday Life*, Harmondsworth: Penguin.

Goldstein J., Freud, A. and Solnit, J. (1980) *Before the Best Interests of the Child*, London. Burnett.

Gorard, S. (1996) 'Three steps to "heaven"? The family and school choice', *Educational Review*, 48, 3, pp. 237–251.

Hacking, I. (1991) 'The making and moulding of child abuse', *Critical Inquiry*, 17, Winter, pp. 253–288.

Hae-Joang, C. (1995) 'The examination war in South Korea', in S. Stephens (ed.) *Childhood and the Politics of Culture*, Princeton, N.J.: Princeton University Press, pp. 141–168.

Hale, C., Farley-Lucas, B. and Tardy, R. (1996) 'Interpersonal conflict from a younger point of view: exploring the perspectives of children', *Qualitative Studies in Education*, 9, 3, pp. 269–291.

Hardy, J. and Vieler-Porter, C. (1990) 'Race, schooling and the 1988 Education Reform Act', in M. Flude and M. Hammer (eds) *The Education Reform Act 1988: its origins and implications*, Basingstoke: Falmer Press, pp. 173–186.

Hargreaves, A. (1994) *Changing Teachers, Changing Times*, London: Cassell.

Hargreaves, A. and Reynolds, D. (1990) 'Decomprehensivisation', in A.

Hargreaves and D. Reynolds (eds) *Educational Policies: controversies and critiques*, Basingstoke: Falmer Press, pp. 1–32.

Harris, C. (1980) 'The changing relationship between family and societal form in western society', in M. Anderson (ed.) *Sociology of the Family* (2nd edition), Harmondsworth: Penguin, pp. 396–413.

Harris, C. C. (1983) *The Family and Industrial Society*, London: Allen & Unwin.

Harris, N. (1991) 'Discipline in schools: the Elton Report', *Journal of Social Welfare Law*, 13, 1, pp. 110–127.

Harris, S. (1994) 'Entitled to what? Control, autonomy in school: a student perspective', *International Studies in the Sociology of Education*, 4, 1, pp. 57–76.

Hawtin, A. and Wise, D. (1997) *Children's Rights: a national and international perspective*, British Council, http://www.

Haywood, C. (1996) 'Sex education policy and the regulation of young people's sexual practice', *Educational Review*, 48, 2, pp. 121–129.

Hendrick, H. (1997) 'Constructions and reconstructions of British childhood: an interpretive survey, 1800 to the present', in A. James and A. Prout (eds) *Constructing and Reconstructing Childhood*, 2nd edition, London: Falmer Press, pp. 34–62.

Hengst, H. (1987) 'The liquidation of childhood: an objective tendency', *International Journal of Sociology* 17, pp. 58–80.

Holt, J. (1975) *Escape from Childhood: the needs and rights of children*, Harmondsworth: Penguin.

Home Office in conjunction with Department of Health (1992) *Memorandum of Good Practice on Videorecording Interviews with Child Witnesses for Criminal Proceedings*, London: HMSO.

Home Office (1998) *Crime and Disorder Act*, London: HMSO.

Hood-Williams, J. (1990) 'Patriarchy for children: on the stability of power relations in children's lives', in L. Chisholm et al. (eds) *Childhood, Youth and Social Change*, London: Falmer Press, pp. 155–170.

Howe, D. 'Modernity, postmodernity and social work', *British Journal of Social Work*, 24, 4, pp. 533–557.

Hughes, M., Nash, T. and Wikely, F. (1994) *Parents and their Children's Schools*, Oxford: Blackwell.

Ivy, M. (1995) 'Have you seen me? Recovering the inner child in late twentieth century America', in S. Stephens (ed.) *Children and the Politics of Culture*, Princeton, N.J.: Princeton Unversity Press, pp. 79–104.

James, A. and Prout, A. (eds) (1990/1997) *Constructing and Reconstructing Childhood*, London: Falmer Press.

James, A., Jenks, C. and Prout, A. (1998) *Theorising Childhood*, Cambridge: Polity Press.

Jeffs, T. (1995) 'Children's educational rights in a new ERA', in B. Franklin (ed.) *Handbook of Children's Rights*, London: Routledge, pp. 25–39.

Jenks, C. (1982) 'Introduction: constituting the child', in C. Jenks (ed.) *The Sociology of Childhood*, London: Batsford, pp. 9–24.

Jenks, C. (1996) *Childhood*. London: Routledge.

John, M. (1995) 'Children's rights in a free market culture', in S. Stephens (ed.)

Children and the Politics of Culture, Princeton, N.J.: Princeton University Press, pp. 105–137.

Johnson, C. 'Freedom in junior schools', in C. B. Cox and A. E. Dyson, *Black Papers in Education*, London: Davis Poynter.

Jonathan, R. (1993) 'Parents' rights in schooling', in P. Munn (ed.) *Parents and Schools*, London: Routledge, pp. 11–26.

Jones, G. and Wallace, C. (1990) 'Beyond individualisation: what sort of social change?', in L. Chisholm et al. (eds) *Childhood, Youth and Social Change*, London: Falmer Press, pp. 134–154.

Kelly, A. V. (1994) *The National Curriculum: a critical review*, London: Paul Chapman.

King, M. (1982) 'Children's rights in education: more than a slogan?', *Educational Studies*, 8, 3, pp. 227–238.

King, P. and Young, I. (1992) *The Child as Client*, Bristol: Family Law.

Kitzinger, J. (1997) 'Who are you kidding? Children, power and the struggle against child abuse', in A. James and A. Prout (eds) *Constructing and Reconstructing Childhood*, 2nd edition, London: Falmer Press, pp. 165–189.

Labour Party (1989) *Meet the Challenge, Make the Change: final report of the Labour Party's policy review for the 1990s*, London: Labour Party.

La Fontaine, J. (1990) *Child Sex Abuse*, Cambridge: Cambridge University Press.

Lasch, C. (1977) *Haven in a Heartless World: the family beseiged*, New York: Basic Books.

Lees, S. (1993) *Sugar and Spice: sexuality and adolescent girls*, London: Penguin.

Lewis, O. (1967) *La Vida: a Puerto Rican family in the culture of poverty*, London: Secker & Warburg.

Lupton, D. and Tulloch, J. (1996) '"All red in the face": students' views on school-based HIV/AIDS and sexuality education', *Sociological Review*, 44, 2, pp. 252–271.

Lyon, C. (1997) 'Children abused within the child care system: do current representation procedures offer the child protection and the family support?', in N. Parton (ed.) *Child Protection and Family Support: tensions, contradiction and possibilities*, London: Routledge, pp. 126–145.

Mac an Ghaill, M. (1994) *The Making of Men: masculinities, sexualities and schooling*, Buckingham: Open University Press.

McKay R. (1973) 'Conceptions of children and models of socialisation', in R. Turner (ed.) *Ethnomethodology*, Harmondsworth: Penguin, pp. 180–193.

Marks, D. (1995) 'Accounting for exclusion: giving a "voice" and producing a "subject"', *Children and Society*, 9, 3, pp. 81–98.

Marshall, T. H. (1950) *Citizenship and Social Class*, Cambridge: Cambridge University Press.

Mayall, B. (1996) *Children, Health and Social Order*, Buckingham: Open University Press.

Meighan, R. (1977) 'The pupil as client: the learner's experience of schooling', *Educational Review*, 29, 2, pp. 123–135.

Melton, G. (1996) 'The improbability of preventing sexual abuse', in D. Willis, E. Holden and M. Rosenberg (eds) *Prevention of Child Maltreatment: developmental and ecological perspectives*, New York: Wiley, pp. 445–482.

Melton, G. and Flood, M. (1994) 'Research policy and child maltreatment: developing the scientific foundation for effective protection of children', *Child Abuse and Neglect*, 18, Supplement 1, pp. 1–28.

Moreno, J. and Torrego, J. (1998) 'Fostering pro-social behaviour in the Spanish school system: the "whole school" response in primary and secondary education', paper presented at European Conference for Educational Research, Ljubjana, September 1998.

Morgan, DHJ. (1985) *The Family, Politics and Social Theory*, London: Routledge & Kegan Paul.

Morris, R., Reid, E. and Fowler, J. (1993) *Education Act 1993: a critical guide*, London: AMA.

Morrow, V. (1996) 'Rethinking childhood dependency: children's contributions to the domestic economy', *Sociological Review*, 44, 1, pp. 58–77.

Murray, C. (1989) 'The underclass', *Sunday Times Magazine*, 26 November, pp. 26–45.

Murray, C. (1990) *The Emerging British Underclass*, London: Institute of Economic Affairs.

Murray, C. (1994) *Underclass: the crisis deepens*, London: Institute of Economic Affairs.

Murray, K. (1995) *Live Television Link*, Edinburgh: Scottish Office.

National Curriculum Council (1992) *Starting out with the National Curriculum*, York: NCC.

O' Brien, M. (1995), 'Allocation of resources in households: children's perspectives', *Sociological Review*, 43, 3, pp. 501–517.

Ofsted (1996) *The Implementation of the Code of Practice for Pupils with Special Educational Needs*, London: HMSO.

O'Keeffe, D. (1994) *Truancy in English Secondary Schools*, London: HMSO.

Oldman, D. (1994) 'Adult/child relations as class relations', in J. Qvortrup et al. (eds) *Childhood Matters: social theory, practice and politics*, Aldershot: Avebury, pp. 153–166.

Olweus, D. (1995) 'Bullying or peer abuse at school: facts and interventions', *Current Directions in Psychological Science*, 4, 6, pp. 196–200.

O'Neill, J. (1982) 'Embodiment and child development: a phenomenological approach', in C. Jenks (ed.) *The Sociology of Childhood*, London: Batsford, pp. 76–86.

Opie, I. and Opie, P. (1969) *Children's Games*, Oxford: Oxford University Press.

Osler, A. (1994) 'The UN Convention on the Rights of the Child: some implications for teacher education', *Education Review*, 46, 2, pp. 141–150.

Owen, R. and Tarr, J. (1998) 'The voices of young people with disability', in C. Holden and N. Clough (eds) *Children as Citizens: education for participation*, London: Jessica Kingsley, pp. 81–94.

Parsons, T. (1954) 'The incest taboo in relation to social structure and the socialisation of the child', *British Journal of Sociology*, 6, 1, pp. 35–68.

Parsons, T. (1965) *Social Structure and Personality*, London: Free Press.

Parsons, T. (1982) 'The socialisation of the child and the internalisation of social value-orientations', in C. Jenks (ed.) *The Sociology of Childhood*, London: Batsford, pp. 139–147.

Parton, N. (1996) 'The new politics of child protection', in J. Pilcher and S. Wagg (eds) *Thatcher's Children?* London: Falmer Press, pp. 43–60.

Parton, N. (1997) 'Child protection and family support: current debates and future prospects', in: N. Parton (ed.) *Child Protection and Family Support: tensions, contradiction and possibilities*, London: Routledge, pp. 1–24.

Paterson, F. (1989) *Out of Place: public policy and the emergence of truancy*, Lewes: Falmer Press.

Pearce, D. (1993) 'Children having children: teenage pregnancy and public policy from the woman's perspective', in A. Lawson and D. Rhodes (eds) *Politics of Teenage Pregnancy*, New Haven: Yale University Press, pp. 174–191.

Phillips, M. (1996) *All Must Have Prizes*, London: Little, Brown & Company.

Platt, E. (1994) 'Children pick up the peace process', *The Independent*, 20 October.

Polanyi, K. (1957) *The Great Transformation*, Boston: Beacon Press.

Pollard, A. (1996) 'Playing the system? Pupil perspectives on curriculum, pedagogy and assessment in primary schools', in P. Croll (ed.) *Teachers, Pupils and Primary Schooling*, London: Cassell, pp. 119–133.

Popenoe, D. (1988) *Disturbing the Nest*, New York: Aldine de Gruyter.

Postman, N. (1982) *The Disappearance of Childhood*, London: Comet.

Prout, A. and Allison, J. (1997) 'A new paradigm for the sociology of childhood? Provenance, promise and problems', in A. James and A. Prout (eds) *Constructing and Reconstructing Childhood* (2nd edition), London: Falmer Press, 7–33.

Qvortrup, J. (1994) 'Childhood matters: an introduction', in J. Qvortrup et al. (eds) *Childhood Matters: social theory, practice and politics*, Aldershot: Avebury, pp. 1–24.

Qvortrup, J. (1997) 'A voice for children in statistical and social accounting: a plea for children's right to be heard', in A. James and A. Prout (eds) *Constructing and Reconstructing Childhood* (2nd edition), London: Falmer Press.

Randolph, M. and Gold, C. (1994) 'Child sexual abuse prevention: evaluation of a teacher training program', *School Psychology Review*, 23, 3, pp. 485–495.

Rispens, J., Aleman, H. and Goudena, P. (1997) 'Prevention of child sexual abuse victimisation: a meta-analysis of school programs', *Child Abuse and Neglect*, 21, 10, pp. 975–987.

Roche, M. (1992) *Rethinking Citizenship*, Cambridge: Polity Press.

Rose, N. (1991) *Governing the Soul: the shaping of the private self*, London: Routledge.

Rufford, N. (1997) 'Parents told to put curfew on tearaways', *The Sunday Times*, 21 September, p. 1.

Saraga, E. (1993) 'The abuse of children', in R. Dallos and E. Mclaughlin (eds) *Social Problems and the Family*, London: Sage, pp. 47–82.

Seabrook, J. (1982) *Working Class Childhood*, London: Gollancz.

Seabrook, J. (1998) 'Children of the market', *Race and Class*, 39, 4, pp. 37–48.

Sears, A. and Hughes, A. (1996) 'Citizenship education and current educational reform', *Canadian Journal of Education*, 21, 2, pp. 123–142.

Sharp, R. and Green, A. (1975) *Education and Social Control*, London: Routledge & Kegan Paul.

Sharp, S. (1996) 'The role of peers in tackling bullying in schools', *Educational Psychology in Practice*, 11, 4, pp. 17–22.

Silcock, P. and Stacey, H. (1997) 'Peer mediation and the cooperative school', *Education 3–13*, 25, 2, pp. 3–8.

Silcock, P., Stacey, H. and Wyness, M. (1996) 'Improving social competence: peer-mediation in Birmingham schools', unpublished paper.

Silverman, D., Baker, C. and Keogh, J. (1998) 'The case of the silent child: advice giving and advice reception in parent–teacher interviews', in I. Hutchby and J. Moran-Ellis (eds) *Children and Social Competence*, London: Falmer Press, pp. 220–240.

Smith, R. (1991) 'Child care: welfare, protection or rights?', *Journal of Social Welfare and Family Law*, 5, pp. 469–481.

Social Exclusion Unit (1998) *Truancy and School Exclusion*, http://www.open.gov.uk/co /sec/trinto.htm; May.

Speir, S. (1982) 'The everyday world of the child', in C. Jenks (ed.) *The Sociology of Childhood*, London: Batsford, pp. 181–188.

Spencer, J. and Flin, R. (1993) *The Evidence of Children*, London: Blackstone.

Stacey, H. and Robinson, P. (1996) *Let's Mediate*, Bristol: Lucky Duck.

Stainton Rogers, W. and Stainton-Rogers, R. (1992) *Stories of Childhood*, London: Harvester Wheatsheaf.

Stephens, S. (1995) 'Introduction: children and the politics of culture in "late capitalism", South Korea' in S. Stephens (ed.) *Childhood and the Politics of Culture*, Princeton, N.J.: Princeton University Press, pp. 1–34.

Sugrue, C. (1997) *Complexities of Teaching: child centred perspectives*, London: Falmer Press.

Suransky, V. (1982) *The Erosion of Childhood*, Chicago: University of Chicago Press.

Taal, M. and Edelaar, M. (1997) 'Positive and negative effects of a child sexual abuse prevention programme', *Child Abuse and Neglect*, 21, 4, pp. 399–410.

Thomas, A. and Dennison, B. (1991) 'Parental or pupil choice – who really decides in urban schools?', *Educational Management and Administration*, 19, 1, pp. 243–249.

Thorne, B. (1993) *Gender Play: girls and boys in school*, Milton Keynes: Open University Press.

Tizard, B. and Hughes, M. (1986) *Young Children Learning: talking and thinking at home and at school*, London: Fontana.

Tutty, L. (1994) 'Developmental issues in young children's learning of sexual abuse prevention concepts', *Child Abuse and Neglect*, 18, 2, pp. 179–192.

United Nations (1989) *The Convention on the Rights of the Child*, Geneva: UN.

Vincent, C. and Tomlinson, S. (1997) 'Home–school relationships: the swarming of disciplinary mechanisms?', *British Educational Research Journal*, 23, 3, pp. 361–377.

Viola, D. (1997) 'Educating children for citizenship', *Ethos P-6*, 2, pp. 6–11.

Vittachi, A. (1989) *Stolen Childhood*, Cambridge: Polity Press.

Wade, B. and Moore, S. (1993) *Experiencing Special Education*, Buckingham: Open University Press.

Walford, G. (1996) 'School choice and the quasi-market', *Oxford Studies in Comparative Education*, 6, 1, pp. 7–16.

Walkerdine, V. (1983) 'Developmental psychology and the child centred pedagogy: the insertion of Piaget into early education', in J. Henriques et al. (eds) *Changing the Subject: psychology, social regulation and subjectivity*, London: Methuen, pp. 153–202.

Warner, M. (1989) *Into the Dangerous World*, London: Chatto.

Waslander, S. and Thrupp, M. (1996) 'Choice, competition and segregation: an empirical analysis of a New Zealand secondary school market', *Journal of Education Policy*, 10, 1, pp. 1–26.

Wattam, C. (1992) *Making a Case in Child Protection*, Harlow: Longman.

Wattam, C. (1997) 'Can filtering processes be rationalised?', in N. Parton (ed.) *Child Protection and Family Support: tensions, contradiction and possibilities*, London: Routledge, pp. 109–125.

West, A., Varlaam, A. and Scott, G. (1991) 'Choice of high schools: pupils' perceptions', *Educational Research*, 33, 3, pp. 205–215.

Wexler, J. (1992) *Becoming Somebody: toward a social psychology of school*, London: Falmer Press.

White, S. (1998) 'Interdiscursivity and child welfare: the ascent and durability of psycho-legalism', *Sociological Review*, 46, 1, pp. 264–292.

Willis, P. (1977) *Learning to Labour*, Aldershot: Avebury.

Winn, M. (1983) *Children without Childhood*, New York: Pantheon.

Woodhead, M. (1997) 'Psychology and the cultural construction of children's needs', in A. James and A. Prout (eds) *Constructing and Reconstructing Childhood*, 2nd edition, London: Falmer Press, pp. 63–84.

Wyness, M. (1994) 'Keeping tabs on an uncivil society: positive parental control', *Sociology*, 28, 1, pp. 193–209.

Wyness, M. (1996a) *Schooling, Welfare and Parental Responsibility*, London: Falmer Press.

Wyness, M. (1996b) 'Policy, protectionism and the competent child', *Childhood: a Global Journal of Child Research*, 3, 4, pp. 431–447.

Wyness, M. (1997) 'Parental responsibilities, social policy and the maintenance of boundaries, *Sociological Review*, 45, 2, pp. 304–324.

Wyness, M. and Silcock, P. (forthcoming) 'Market values, primary schooling and the pupils' perspective', in R. Gardner (ed.) *Values and the Curriculum*, London: Institute of Education, pp. 74–92.

Index